OrangeBooks Publication

Smriti Nagar, Bhilai, Chhattisgarh - 490020

Website: **www.orangebooks.in**

First Edition, 2021

ISBN: 978-93-92878-55-8

The opinions/ contents expressed in this book are solely of the author and do not represent the opinions/ standings/ thoughts of OrangeBooks.

500 Magical Spell Infused *Affirmations*

The Ultimate Step By Step Guide To Get Your Ex Back

•••••

Chirasree Banerjee

OrangeBooks Publication

www.orangebooks.in

500 Magical Spell Infused Affirmations : The Ultimate Step By Step Guide To Get Your Ex Back

This is the "How To Get Your Ex Back" blueprint.

This book has proven strategies on how you can finally get your ex back. The 500 affirmations are subdivided into 50 stages and are spell infused. This book is written with an intension to guide you through the process to ultimately take you to the vortex where you have already received your manifestation.

About The Author

Chirasree Banerjee (aka Chirasree Bandyopadhyay) is a Christ Consciousness Spiritual Teacher, quantum spiritual scientist & has invented plethora of unique quantum modalities. She also has won the WEAA award in 2020 for her outstanding performance as an entrepreneur. She was also recently featured in Daily Hunt for being one of the Foxclues India Top 100 Women 2021 . Chirasree in fact recently got interviewed by Stroyiaan .She's the founder of the company Quantum Dynamic 8. You can find out more about her work & lifestyle at www.quantumdynamic8.com.

Get Your Ex Back is her soul aligned purpose that she's currently working on. As a certified student of none other than Tony Robbins & Dean Graziosi, she truly loves entrepreneurship with her heart and soul. She specialises in core belief clearing , quantum integration, shift consciousness and manifestation. She's an emotional intelligence expansion expert and has created a revolution in the new age high vibrational self help spiritual transformation industry. She's well known across the globe and is certified by many renowned professionals like Tony Robbins, Dean Graziosi, Access Consciousness, Infinite Healing, Nitin Mohan Lal, Joe

Vitale to name some of the great teachers. She's also a reiki level IV master, joyous body protocol practitioner, advanced law of attraction and core belief clearing practitioner certified by Joe Vitale .

What Chirasree Banerjee loves about her work is that , she gets to meet like minded beings for her profession everyday, who are constantly focussed on self growth and development ,always choosing to learn, grow & expand – to contribute from the best version of themselves. Resourcefulness, ability to identify and grasp the right opportunities at the right time, is the secret behind your achievements. The magic beneath and surmounting everything is God

Be Proud To Be Who You Are Not Ashamed To Be How Someone Else Sees You

It's neither about the red pill or the blue pill, it's about taking the chill pill. That's Chirasree's philosophy. Create your own new set of standards .Create your own new set of norms. Don't be triggered by what they say, trigger them by standing in your own truth for a change. Hone the wisdom and riches of your soul. You are a powerful being. The choice of your destiny is not separate from the path that you have chosen to follow. You are destined to always be where you are at. The next moment you can be in any other parallel reality and that is also your choice. To shift parallel realities is to feel that as if you already have what you seek and know it - so literally that you can choose that as if in the physicality. Pretend beyond what feels delusional, then transcend & surpass the feeling of delusion, overwriting it with such faith & determination, that as if you can feel that your manifestation is here in the physical reality. Therefore immediately that instantaneously can affect the outer reality to align for you , always absolutely synced to where you are at that "now" moment ,within. You attract what you expect. You expect what you feel & think that you truly deserve. The inner and outer reality are aligning now. To the extent to which you are feeling ready, also to that extent you will feel destined. To be aware that it's destined is also to know that it's meant to happen. The more you feel that you have received it , the more you will feel it's destined to happen & the more you will see possibilities showing up for you. Jump in the joy of knowing that you are destined to have it so you can have it now ,when you hold that feeling - you need to feel that it's destined & that will create the needful pressure in your chest centre , to prepare your heart for the manifestation. It's the vortex where after preparation of your heart to perceive – you reach the consciousness to receive. The vortex is the core most inner lining of your chest centre through the resistances where you reach . The resistances have perfectly prepared you to reach that point, absolutely in divine synchronicity, this is where you just know that your manifestation is about to happen or show up for you- much literally! In this knowing you breakthrough from the vortex to quantum leap to the parallel vibration or reality where it's done. Meanwhile it's taken care of and happens in a perfect order. Get your ex back is a process, a path of faith belief , determination and resiliency of that of a true lover. This sequence of the path ultimately generates the feeling in you, where you finally feel at the core that now you so deserve it.

Therefore you'd just work from the state of humility then and work on feeling more worthy and deserving of receiving it (your manifestation) within. The more you can gear the strength to feel worthy at the core of your being that you have received it, dropping every resistance – the faster the magic will show up for you or align you to your destiny. Choose the thought that it's possible and it has happened for you. You feel worthy and thus it has shown up for you & you feeling worthy is an indication to the universe that you are ready to receive your manifestation. God will never leave you overwhelmed, God's path to miracle is very natural. In that state of flowing beautifully in the course of knowing, you'll manifest your ex back – you will actually end up manifesting. Just trust the process.God is beautiful. It's a game of conscience purification ultimately .

At the age of 27 she has done 40+ modalities and Chirasree started her business at the age of 22 only. She started channelling God since she was 12 years old and that's when God first revealed to her the idea of life purpose. That's how out of nowhere she learnt that word. When she was 9 years old God told her that there is an important mission for which she has come to earth. Now she feels it's to spread these words of wisdom and awareness that she experiences. This is the mission – a spiritual warfare, to fight for your rights & choose to design a reality according to your preference. Always being a very bright student, a person full of heart and soul, she has always lived a life connected to the soul. During the time of ascension, as a super nova old soul, she feels enormously blessed. She says it's a blessing we are on this planet during this time. The idea of love, relationship, good , bad that we have as standards now – we are going through a deeper purification of those ideas to open our minds more to truly allow ourselves to be who we are authentically meant to be. So if you have picked up this book , you are a kindred spirit. Know we're all in this together. We will get through this. Everything is a mind construct, if nothing existed, nothing mattered , what would you want to create in that white slate? She is indeed a gift of God, an earth angel, here to create new norms of her own for her own personal life and to motivate others too to implement these strategies & apply them in their life so they too can live life on their own terms authentically. She's pulled to manifest a new reality where beyond every barrier and labels, all true lovers have united in harmony and are receiving the kind of love that they desire beyond the threat of what will people say? We already are there in her physical reality. She is living from that state of consciousness and is raising the collective frequency as a lightworker for more people to unify here where love is all that's. Along with her soul tribe, who are also free spirits , she is transcending to shift this awareness at the root of collective frequency so more souls can wake up to choose this love. She has courses that plethora of professionals are practicing today ,worldwide , who are certified by Chirasree Banerjee. She is a coach, author and the unique quantum spiritual scientist who is magical in a very unique way. This is her fourth book after Diary Of A Stoner (2016), Offers To Malik :The Journey Within. Based On The Twin Flames

Journey (2019), Chronological Remembrance - A Guide
To Inner Child Healing & Integration (2021)

Book Synopsis

I reprogram your subconscious mind with this affirmative book which will be taking you on a journey within and this book also comes with many more magical tools that are waiting to be read & implemented by you in your magically real life. It's the book where God talks to you through every layer of your emotion to help you to transcend every barricade holding you back to manifest the unseen to be seen now. I am just a medium , a channel of God. Thank you God.

Introduction

I believe after all these years it is still possible. Even though I can't believe I can really get back with my ex. I have a deep desire in my heart though but I wonder if it's possible or not. I have tried to move on, I have loved my self enough to let them go but something just keeps bringing me back to this love, to this feeling.

I have met a thousand soulmates but nothing feels like this love. This is the ultimate form of love which wasn't discovered perhaps before I lost it

In every part of my being, if there is any wish and desire I have that's to be with the love of my life. Somehow beyond the land of impossibilities, the many resistances, it has already happened, in a parallel reality. Doesn't it sound so familiar?

Now I choose to turn these pages to explore the absolute magic to fill in every part of my being. It does feel so good to have gifted myself such a pretty, aesthetically refined, beautifully rich ,adorable, informative and a full of knowledge book that has completely given a new meaning to my life already. This book is a great contribution to the society. The book is that book which always makes me feel that I am here,now. It's a part & parcel of my everyday life. It has given me a purpose, it has given me the zeal to rekindle my spirit of being .

These will be your words as you keep coming back to this book in your journey of reconciliation.

This book has been divided into 50 stages to help you to reconcile with your ex . Each affirmation will penetrate against your negative core beliefs in that space which you have cleared with the guidance you have received from my previous book , Chronological Remembrance - A Guide To Inner Child Integration & Healing.

Many of you that are reading this book have probably done my courses too or have taken spells from me or is my VIP client who I've worked with in the past or is working with currently. Thank you for choosing to read this book . Thank you for your constant & endless support. This book can also be your oracle medium – a way to check where you are vibrationally in this very moment. You can also make it a medium to talk to your specific person. Just randomly open the book and the page you land up in, that's got the message that God has for you for what your specific person has to tell you now – through God. God can talk to you through anything. It's God who is talking to you through everything and everyone. All the signs and synchronicities are but from God.

Even though you don't see a possibility .Just know everything is happening to create a possibility for you to have your dream come true. It's not wrong to choose to stand apart, you are choosing to stand apart because this is just one life. You would not want to regret that you didn't listen to your heart and a part of you was yearning be with your ex. Give yourself a chance to bravely invest the gift of manifestation into something that truly matters to you without bothering about what people have to say about your choice. You didn't come to this world to live for others. You are not here to please people. You are here to live life on your own terms and will to feel good. Go out of your comfort zone and take the risk to believe it's possible. In regards to your individual situation, you'll receive more clarity and can see the how it's going to be possible, if you choose to persist. It's already done. Don't give up on your dreams and desire. Beyond all that can be seen is the unseen. Remember it's the unseen that manifests into being seen. You can read the book anytime and as many times that you want.

More you read and rewire your subconscious mind, the more aligned you start to get to the process of self transformation & start to level up. You begin to attract synchronicities and catch the momentum which leads to attracting your ex back. "Reasons come first, answers come second."- Jim Rohn. Write down 10 reasons why you deserve and thus should receive your manifestation. Tony Robbins says ; when you are sure of something, the actions that you take come from a place where you give all of yourself to it. However until you are sure you will be scared. To be courageous in a situation doesn't mean you lack fear but you do it anyway with the fear when you are coming from the frequency of courage. Take the risk to believe that you have received your manifestation. The exact version of your ex that you desire, you have manifested them. It has happened exactly as you desire. Do you choose to give yourself the permission to receive the desired version of your ex that you always preferred the most? Will you not regret not giving this chance to yourself? Wouldn't it be deeply disappointing to retrospect back & find out that you didn't give yourself the chance for maybe what will people say? Don't worry about what will others think. It's about the two of you. Do you choose to give yourself the permission to receive commitment from your ex how you desire? You deserve it and so you have received it.

This book can be your Oracle Medium too by the way. How?

Open the Book on Random Page and Start Reading..

You will surely resonate , find it relatable to your current life situation , experiences & wisdom. Of course you will get the absolute clarity in your current reality in coherence to your exact vibrational frequency, needed to propel forward at this point.

Always in the area of discomfort in your heart where you are desiring the union – from that place read this book , from that place you are flowing and creating the momentum for what you are manifesting in life. It's in that feeling you just have to truly know that you have manifested your desire

The words on the page will cast a spell in your state of consciousness imprinting the intension associated to the words in you. You'll feel more vibrant, energetic and soulful every time that you read this book . This is going to be your best friend from now onwards , the ultimate self help guide that you were always looking for – in path of manifesting your specific person . Meanwhile if the numbers on this book are pulling you, look within, around, or on the internet, in books, in the offline world, in your very room- for meaning and signs, God is talking to us through everything all the time. In the heart of our presence, we are now present and changing that feeling that you feel now in your heart to how you want to feel, that change in the feeling shifts the momentum and causes magic to happen as it shifts our core frequency & vibration , the momentum simultaneously changes. Manifestation is absolutely real . Your work is to have faith and filling up the gap between you can and can't believe that you are the person who is already married to your ex. Getting your ex to call you is a short term goal but to think about being married to them already is a long term goal. It's in that state of consciousness, your belief system generates a frequency which leads to creation of incidents which lead to getting your ex back. Whatever you experience , you have imagined it first in your mind unconsciously. Manifestation is also deliberate creation. It's about giving yourself the permission to feel deserving enough to allow yourself to receive the commitment that you desire from your ex in the way that you seek. I intend that you have already received the commitment exactly how you desire from your ex.

When you go to the gym, have you noticed that after a couple of days, how you lose the motivation that you had initially when you decided to join the gym? However when you book a personal trainer who keep you accountable, you do the work, you take it seriously. This is because you constantly receive the motivation or push to keep going. What manifests is consistency in the momentum. A coach does the same to keep you accountable, a coach constantly remind you the reality of manifestation and that how you are creating your reality.

This keeps you in the momentum to keep going to know that you already have received your manifestation. You can read about the plethora of success stories of my clients who got back their ex at www.quantumdynamic8.com. What gave them success was choosing to adhere to the momentum to keep going and believing that it's already done.

Here's a beautiful contribution from Magda for this book. Thank you Magda for choosing to contribute to my book.

"My journey goes like this,

I was extremely uncertain about my dream of marrying my twin flame yet I had this one thing called FAITH that it is certain to happen. I haven't spoken to my TF since two years along with that were many misunderstandings. With full faith in Allah, I asked to simply show me a way to clear my obstacles and one day that supreme heard me, by sending me her page on Facebook while I was surfing on newsfeed, yet I was short of money to pay…I was waiting for my salary yet somewhere I was disappointed that I wouldn't make up because of my family commitments, there too Allah heard me, he made my arrangements is such superb way that it didn't hurt neither my family commitments nor my desire to take up the manifest your SP course.

Then I knew, it was Allah's consciousness who gave me a call to approach this lovely girl named Chirasree, I religiously heard her pre requisite videos and her book before our one on one session. Chirasree has been so friendly and open to talk my heart out wherein I was wondering whether I am in real or in my dreams, I felt so much light after her magical scripts, personalised videos and a beautiful yet powerful sigil.

She is always there for you anytime, I even type to her first whenever any major chirp or atrocity I face, she has ready solutions for you. She even makes you feel so easy that no problem is too hard that you need rocket science to crack.

After, I completed my course with her, a few days later, I saw the engagement of my juniors who are undoubtedly made for each other and one of the most outspoken love stories in my medical college where I pursued my MBBS, I was totally inspired with their engagement and I decided to manifest the same with my TF on my birthday this year, You won't believe, I have started seeing many amazing signs, I started living in the end and the process of this manifestation grew stronger and stronger. Meanwhile in this process, me along with my family were diagnosed with COVID this late August where my father ought to have immediate ICU admission. The whole month of September went so rough and at last, my father passed away..it was a sad ending, yet a new beginning happened, my TF spoke to me on the third of the mourning, gave me condolence. It was a sweet talk and I fell for him again.

Waiting for more…Thank you Chirasree for so much support and love.Love you to the moon and back sister

With Love,
Magda "

Here's another phenomenal contribution from Manish

Thank you Manish for choosing to contribute these words

I remember how I came across Chirasree while scrolling randomly on Instagram. I messaged her after checking some of her posts and that's when my journey started with Chirasree. I can talk about most of the courses from Chirasree but I would be specific to two of very important courses which are not estimated as it deserves. As in I feel Chirasree must endorse them in a way they deserve

Attracting SP (Special / Specific Person)

So if you think it's just about attracting that one specific person then you are underestimating it too. The layers that are worked make you so powerful that you will not only attract SP but anything you want to. The power or the belief that one gets after doing this course is on another level. You can attract any thing you want, not only SP. The course is a journey itself. The journey where in you have realisation of many things and with guidance from Chirasree it becomes very easy. She reaches to the point that needs attention and enables you to achieve your manifestation. You will feel amazing light and sense amazing energy while doing this course. The course enables and empowers individuals to achieve their manifestation and wrongly called by founder that it just about attracting SP

QECAT

So when you have a higher purpose you tend to look for it and the right frequency or vibration sends you to the right place. I have come to Chirasree to work out on something else and I end getting these amazing lessons. The moment I started doing the course, it took me to the various places and times. From the inner child healing to quantum integration to self love, this course has everything.

In 2020, Jan and July I completed 3 courses from another reputed organization and it cost more than 60k.

However QECAT offered by Chirasree had every topic what was covered in all of these courses and I just paid 11k for this course with lifetime access to the course. I learnt valuable lessons here and now I can say that I am a step closer to my higher purpose. Also, QECAT takes you and your spirituality on a different level.

Suggestion: you do QECAT for sure even if you don't choose other courses and thank me later.

I am still drowning in this beautiful experience and what makes it wonderful is that I have a spiritual guru for lifetime.

1. You can drop message to Chirasree and it gets addressed

2. She can help you pushing in right energy.

3. Her voice is magical. There is something special about it for sure.

4. There are so many points to write and I am short of space.

Here are wise words of Kinjal about her journey

Where do I begin from, meeting Chirasree on Instagram by chance was something that I was looking for since long. I had been working on myself and beyond the point where I was stuck, i needed someone higher then myself to help me and that's when I came across her. It was no less than a miracle in itself. I could connect to her at a different level spiritually and grasp at the way how she worked with me totally in the school of manifestation where within two weeks I could get back my twin flame who wasn't in my contact for past 8 months. But I also knew my journey was not complete so I still work with her and breaking my barriers to manifest the kind of life I want in which she is with me helping me in this journey of my inner work. There is nothing great then listening to her "love that part" Which works wonders for me. Her cause to make people reach their apex of their potential and never ending zest to find issues inside you to work upon is amazing. Never found a guru like her and glad to have her by my side always. I know I'll get married soon and it will be entirely her efforts in breaking all my myths and barriers and resistances.

Thank you for taking the time to choose to contribute your precious words in my book. I'm beyond grateful for your presence in my life. Thank you for your constant support and love

Mileage Of Your Momentum

The mileage of your momentum strengthens as you gain more surety. Understanding that manifestation really works, you create your reality, the surrounding physical circumstances and available evidences don't matter. What matters is what you resonate to or relate to. This is when you start getting into the vortex of allowance and receiving. Each time you feel like you are unable to allow yourself to receive the manifestation, just drop the tension by choosing to detach from the sensation that thought is creating in your chest centre. The moment you drop the tension, you land up in the vortex of creation . As long as there is the tension, there's a need to control. The moment you drop the tension, you realise you live in an infinite realm of infinite possibilities where nothing is right or wrong. The tension is the pressure that you are feeling around your heart space. It's about dropping that thrust you feel as if much physically around your heart space. When you succeed to do so, you catch the flow state to call in abundance of joy, love and serendipity to flow through you. However it starts with releasing the thrust and acknowledging a reality devoid of it - to allow a reality of magic in. Anything is possible and it's a matter of choice, it's that tight tension which is making you feel like you have a resistance in your way. The moment you drop the tension , you move immediately back to this realm of infinity . It's in this realm , you manifest & the magic happens.

Just feel your feeling, release the tension , choose the outcome of desire and thank God for teleporting you to the vortex where you already have your manifestation. A vortex is the point where the pressure is built for you to gear the emotional stability to jump into the desired frequency or preferred reality. You are becoming the person who has received their manifestation. Anything that does not allow you that is a tension creating that resistance. You just have to drop the tension and know you have received your manifestation exactly how you desire. The breakthrough is your divine birthright. You release the tension by releasing the emotional pull causing a tightness in your chest centre that you feel from the thought of it'll not happen exactly the way you desire, by changing it to it'll happen exactly the way you desire - immediately invites a sense of assuring relaxation in your heart space. Change the meaning that you are assigning to the uneasiness within and you'll immediately be out of it.

Resonance if is adhered to "I'm so sad, my ex is not in my life. I'm so shattered. " This resonance/that which you relate to it (it being that you are so heartbroken) makes you focus on everything around that gives you more reasons to be sad. You come across songs, social media posts to everything that makes you resonate to that frequency more. The reticular activating system(RAS) is responsible for making your brain focus on everything that's most important to you at that point of time. If you are interested in real estate and you've gone to a cafe, on a table far away if a group of people are discussing about real estate, your focus will go there . This is because RAS ensures that it focuses on things that are important to you. This is how synchronicities occur. When you continue to feed your subconscious mind and deliberately force yourself to believe that you are already with your ex, the pressure created by the deliberate creation, enhances the momentum. The more deliberately you believe, the momentum receives the mileage to keep going. It's in this mileage of faith and deliberate force of belief that strengthens the momentum, a frequency is generated in this process which affects the current resonance and shifts it to a new resonance where you can believe that your ex has already shown up. It's in that belief, you continue to gear more momentum and with God and in God, in God's magical love, the momentum continues to accentuate to ultimately create the synergy to create a simulation to bring everything to a frequency where you can just naturally believe that it's done, your ex has shown up. This is when you live in the end. It's in this phase everything shifts to redesign the bridge of events to unify you to the vortex where you are the one who has received the commitment from your ex exactly how you desire.

The quality in a sound of being deep, full, and reverberating is the definition of resonance. Here the quality of the sound knowing of the fact that you are already with your ex has to be deep, full and reverberating. The reverberation will create the momentum which when reaches the amplitude of being the frequency where you have received your manifestation. That amplification shall show up as result in the physical reality. This is how manifestation works and how the result shows up. This is applicable for mechanism of machines to sound recording to chemical experiments to quantum physics dynamics to manifesting anything to building momentum for success . It's all connected. It's life. We are streaming from the same source. Everything manifests or shows up or processes or formulates as an extension of this very internal processing. It's all about the resonance. When the core resonance shifts, surrounding energetic frequency gets affected, that effect causes the result to show up. This is how your ex is going to show up/manifest.

After you finish reading this book, you'll reach a state that when any fear or limiting beliefs come up, you can just remind yourself that you create your reality, so whatever you are experiencing, is an amplification of your resonance. So just by working on your limiting beliefs (which you'll learn to, in this book) you can change the resonance that you are vibing at now or at any point in time to create a reality where you have manifested your ex back. It all starts in the mind.

Here's a simple exercise that I learnt from my teacher Tony Robbins. Stand up and stretch your right hand outwards , pointing your index finger towards the direction that you are looking at. Now try to bend your hand backwards in the same position , and see how far you can stretch your hand. Now come back again, close your eyes and imagine bending your hand in your mind. Go as far as you can in your mind. Now imagine the same three times. Now again start from the beginning, stretch your hand outwards to point your index finger towards where you are looking at , now try bending & stretching your hand backwards, this time you'll be able to stretch even more further than the first time. This is because we have created limiting beliefs in the mind about what we can do and what we cannot do. If we get stuck in those stories, we will create a reality in coherence to those stories. This is why old story needs to change to a new story when you are manifesting. The moment you went far off in your mind to imagine that you can stretch your hand backwards even further, you succeeded immediately because you believed you can. It all starts in the mind. When you can imagine it in the mind, you can create it in your reality. It starts in the mind. You can have the exact version of your ex that you desire, exactly how you want. The very vibration of your reality in which you desire to be with your ex , you are self allowance away to give yourself the chance/permission slip to receive this commitment that you desire. Do you choose to give yourself the permission slip now? Magic is real. Meanwhile I know this is how many of you are feeling at this point of time "Although I have started to feel that world is not a safe place." Whenever you are tensed, you are creating a resistance, the moment you drop the tension, you allow perfect alignment and a constant flow state. "The world is out there to get me. Everything in this world is against me. This world is a terrible place to be in. No one really gets me. It's like I have reached the end of this world after this break up and I make sense to no one. I feel like my situation is exceptionally the tough one. I feel like there's no way out of here. I feel like I really want to be loved. I feel like I really want to be chosen. I feel like I really want to have my set of people. I feel like I want to be understood by those people who really get me – who really know what it feels to go through this. I really want to be chosen. I really want to belong. I want to find my tribe, my kind of people who really get me and are connected to my soul. They share similar frequencies to my soul. I want to meet that version of my partner in a parallel reality where they treat me like I want to be treated." This is your current resonance formed by the tension of resistance. Whenever you feel anxious/

resistance that's because there is a lot of tension that you feel. Each pinching sensation is a tension

The moment you drop the tension, the resistance goes away and as the resistance goes away, you'll get into the vortex where the manifestation happens .

Therefore try to focus on dropping the tension. Understand that the resistance is there in the first place because of the tension. If the tension is taken away, the resistance will go away. The moment you release the tension, there's a transcendental shift where you have received the breakthrough.

Isn't this also your voice ? "I want to be just like everyone who receive their manifestation. I want to be with the version of the love of my life where they are aligned to a frequency by the virtue of which they are resonating in perfect harmony to where I live. My partner is meeting me here and is aligning to my perspective of resonance. Everything is energy. The soul is but just light and energy so it can instantaneously transmute in any state when free of resistance. With every catalysis perfectly designed I have manifested this path. Now I remember how finally my phone began to ring and I heard exactly what I wanted to hear from my partner. It all worked out suddenly in this process."

Applying radical self love is to choose that you are worthy of receiving the exact kind of reality that you desire to now show up in your immediate reality & knowing that it's possible. You deserve it.

So The Many Benefits Of Reading This Book Are

Just by changing your current feelings (the state of emotion that you are in NOW) , your hormones shift, your hormones give the signals to your muscles to relax and the blood circulation rate relaxes when the speed of the blood passing through your arteries , veins and capillaries balance out. So your heart muscles can relax now as vena cava gives the signal to do so.

In that state of consciousness you experience a shift/ change of your emotional state of consciousness/the shield of feelings holding you back fall and shifts as you read the book. The book is scientifically designed step by step to make you understand by integrating your logic – with the understanding that how it's happening .

Your muscles relax and you come out of anxiety and find the clarity to move forward with ease, grace and joy. This book is written after many group and online one on one successful case studies. I have playlists, highlights and timeline filled with success stories on my YouTube, Instagram & Facebook respectively. This book is strategically planned in order to bring out the best in you. This is that book which takes you to a consciousness where just alone by reading it - you catch that energy frequency where you finally have the strength to believe fearlessly that you have received your manifestation. In other words you feel enough clarity now to move into the state where you feel at ease to catch the momentum of your emotions that you would feel when you are moving forward to receive your desire and also where you have received it already. It is done. So it is. Thus it shall be. Amen

No matter what you have done or your person has done to you, if you want a union or not - regardless of that everyone deserves to be forgiven at the core. Choose to know that you are worthy of receiving the kind of forgiveness that lets you feel that you deserve this relationship now. If you have to forgive them, then do so. They too deserve to receive this forgiveness. Upon receiving the forgiveness , now choose to allow the core aspect of this relationship and the idea of the two of you coming together, to receive the forgiveness to now give yourself the second chance . Forgive the idea of not giving or receiving the second chance. Forgive the judgement surrounding the idea of receiving the second chance . Forgive the feeling of feeling non deserving of this second chance, you'll naturally move into a state now where you will feel that you have received this second chance now. It's time now. You are the one who has successfully manifested this relationship once again and you are in this relationship now with the love of your life. You are committed now to the person of your dreams. You are in an absolutely harmonious relationship with the love of your life and of your dreams. Your dream has finally come true and now you are in the exact kind of relationship that you always wanted & that too with the person you wanted to be in a relationship with.

You can MANIFEST EVERYTHING no matter WHAT.

In this new state of consciousness that you've reached - break the barricades to formulate to become a frequency where you become one with your desire . This book can miraculously shift you to that frequency revealing and healing all your blocks instantly. This is a magical book that you are reading and you also have manifested this at the same time, somewhere deep down

This is that one thing which could really resolve it all and finally would tell you how you would get your manifestation done, where you were going wrong and what exactly were you missing out on . This is that missing link that you were waiting for

When you hold the frequency of that your manifestation is done that leads to you becoming the vibration that you would be when you have had your manifestation manifested. This leads to finally opening the portal to welcome your

MANIFESTATION.

When you persist on holding on to the feeling that you have what you want – it manifests. This book takes you to a state where you become the feeling you would feel when you have your manifestation - instantly and permanently. Nothing is set in stone, life is unpredictable. Energy is always changing. It's all about the NOW moment.

No matter where you are – based on your vibration in the now moment, you can choose to feel how you want to feel. That feeling when you hold onto - you manifest more of that feeling. So hold on to the feeling that you are the one who has manifested their partner exactly the way they desire. You are loved . This book is not only going bro help you to attract your ex back but you can read this book to rekindle a spark between you and your current partner too

You can come back to each stage whenever you feel that base emotion / name of the stage

Affirm: "Exactly how I desire in that way my person has showed up in my reality. Exactly how I want in that way in every realm of my life, everything has worked out. No matter what I have been through, no matter what insult I had to endure, my person is now realising that they could have behaved so much better with me. My person really loves and adores me. The separation is making my person realise that I deserved to be treated better and upon knowing and realising that my person is thinking of a new beginning with me. They look at their current reality and everything looks like an illusion to them. They are ready to let go of it all to choose me at the very core of their being. All the grudges, barriers, unforgiving uneasiness are coming from a state of ultimately holding on to this pain that this relationship didn't work out the way they desired it to in the past. They are realising that it's a blessing that both of you are still alive and life is not over yet so both of you can let go of the dis-ease and are choose the cure. The cure is unconditional love. Finally you are choosing the core aspect in you, of them to choose to love you now, in the way that you desire. You are completely letting go of the idea of the person that they were. You realise that lead to the idea of who they are now. You are letting go of your idea of who they are now. You are choosing the idea of a completely different reality where you are with the idea of a new version of them. They are very different from who they are now and they are choosing you completely. They have agreed to give you the kind of commitment that you desire. At the core you are now choosing that seriously this is happening and that's leading to the breakthrough and the ideal version of them is here now, ready to show up."

You will receive your manifestation when your thoughts, feelings, emotions, belief, behaviour, action, understanding, knowing & being have to aligned in oneness in every angle

What you just read , how can you apply that?

Thought – You are with your partner now. You have reconciled.

Feeling – You feel like you are with your partner now

Emotion – If you were on a stage & was an actor - and had you been asked to bring up emotions to feel that as if you really have your manifestation manifested now, what emotions would be generated in you?

Belief – You can believe by literally generating the emotions that as if you are now with your partner - beyond the fear of your dreams getting scattered, it has happened.

Behaviour – Now that you completely believe you have your manifestation in the core of your heart / in the centre of your chest space, how does this feeling make you behave from the core of the conscience of your conscience?

You must feel you deserve it in your conscience until you reach this stage , keep rehearsing. Choosing to have a manifestation coach at this stage accelerates the process & help you to keep up with the momentum. Releasing the limiting negative core beliefs is of utmost necessity at this point.

Before you start implementing this, ensure you don't reach out to your ex . Wait for them to reach out to you. Don't chase after them or message them. The needy energy actually slows down the process. My clients often come back in contact , to again come and tell me that their person is ignoring them, all over again. Each and every time my answer has been one and the same that they need to direct that love back within. A great hack to love yourself is to simply love the not so good feeling you are feeling now and to be unconditionally present with it by allowing it to have what it desires - non judgementally & unafraid. Change the meaning you assign to the triggers. Shift the thought of I don't get a good vibe to this is just a thought, I'm shifting it now, I believe that I am now getting & feeling the best vibe. This is how you quantum leap states, immediately.

Get over the old beliefs as how things are with your ex or what had happened. I know it's not easy so I have dedicated the first half of the book to work on core beliefs and self concept. After going through the series of layers of blocks that I have shared which I've seen universally present in my clients , I can assure you that as you read them you'll heal. The book is written with that intension. It's in a scientific method , the book has been written , much very strategically. Being a Christ Consciousness Teacher, I love the teachings and studies of Krishna Consciousness as well. Even though my yogic path has to do with integrating molecules in the quantum field. However the source of all that's, it's beyond science. It's an energy that can change the most agnostic person to holistic. The light of pure consciousness of the conscience streams from the very source and the source is all that's.

It's here, there, everywhere and all that's. It's beyond what is what has been and what will ever be. It's a power that has created all of us, this entire cosmos, galaxies and stars. It's the life in all that's, it's what is alive. In it's essence, with it , we can manifest anything. We also call it GOD.

I have seen success stories where husbands changed their mind about giving divorce to their wives, I have seen lovers reunite after years, I have had that experience in my personal life too , even I don't know how many success stories I've had till date. I have seen plethora of third parties getting removed , relationships finding the spark back after years. People quitting alcohol and drugs after years of addiction, people healing from mid life crises & sex addiction. I have heard of millions of stories where people came out of cancer & other deadly diseases , I know people who have come out of ventilation to have had oxygen levels get normal. I have seen literal miracles. I talk to God since I was seven years old and unconsciously obviously I manifested that. You too can. Just choose to consciously talk to God. Allow Him to be your best friend. We are always manifesting our realities into existence. I have seen those people get married who came to me with blocks in their path. I have attended marriages that I manifested, even the exact dates for. Manifestation is a path that flows from a state of alignment and surety effortlessly. Focus on your alignment and your belief system manifests. The manifestation is already done. You are already there. You are getting vibrationally ready to see it.

I have seen miraculous cases shift in just a day. I have seen my clients have magnificent breakthroughs after breakthroughs where they have even come out of anxiety in just a few days whereas, when they've struggled with that for years. I have seen people become independent and Quantum Dynamic 8 has empowered many to find their true path, learn skills to start their own business. I have received my manifestations time and again. After the most complicated state I thought I was in, my ex came back several times in last few years but I dared to let him go because I was not choosing to manifest the version that had shown up. I let him go by loving him and setting the boundaries that were needed to ensure I am choosing my inner peace , ideology and self love first . I dared to risk the concept of not being just friends with my ex. I chose to let it all go. When I initially let it all go, it was coming from the faith in the intensity of my love for him, later on it was faith in the power of manifestation from where I later began to let go. It was more effortless . You can't ever mess up your manifestation. What you desire is desiring you. Manifestation is a two way process where you meet your manifestation, halfway. Manifesting your ex will need you to let go of them many times and choosing the inner feeling that you are feeling now . Don't get caught up by the third dimensional reality at all. I have manifested relationships with celebrities - multiple times and have been and are grateful to always manifest money and abundance that is always coming my way easily and effortlessly and each of my transactions always lead to mutual benefit. I manifest knowledge , great teachers, courses , information and wisdom everyday. I have worked with over 1000+ clients who I manifested, in last four years. I have been manifesting my business to level up more and more in every way, everyday. I have manifested this state where I'm writing this book from the perspective & knowing that it is the next bestseller.

I manifest everything into my existence consciously and live a life in the now moment, where every action within and without are synced. When I feel inspired I take actions to take the leap of faith within or I take quantum leap where I just absolutely believe a reality to be true when I'm completely out of the resistances within, emotionally. It's when I can absolutely believe in something to be completely true. That's when I immediately shift to become that and my immediate reality becomes a match to it. I am living this life forever and it has always worked for me. In recent years I figured I always had been manifesting deep quantum knowledge from the quantum field. The name of my company Quantum Dynamic 8 , also was a manifestation, my courses where I teach how to shift mind dimensions and open portals, I have manifested it all. I just manifest quantum physics based information so many times throughout the day. Your inner realisation when match up with the available information, you realise and have a wisdom integrated. That integration activates the portal to receive more downloads. I always get healthier and my skin glows more,it is just a choice which I know I absolutely deserve, I believe it is possible, so I know I can have them and I simply know them into being. My life is only getting better & better everyday and it's my choice. I chose not to be a spiritual sheep but stand out to choose the kind of dynamic in a relationship that I prefer. People have told me possessiveness is control. I changed the belief in me to realise that the idea of control being controlling itself is another man made limiting narrow minded belief in the first place.It's easy to call a girlfriend controlling and jealous but hitting on her boyfriend or breaking their relationship boundaries, is also an act of desperation and extreme characterlessness smeared with unmet sexual thirst with lack of integrity and unhealed codependency . To judge, it could thus raise wars. As it just did in just a contradictory statement highlighting two sides of the coin of judgement, in a situation. So best is to just be who you prefer, unapologetically & non judgementally without trying to fix others. Live & let others live. Manifest the desired reality vibrationally in your heart. The rest will fall in place safely with perfection. The same control that cages one, another person who likes BDSM enjoys that. Now everything that's controlling and bad to one, might be the bad ass, very lit thing for another. We live in a free world, hone your feelings to freely feel and make choices that you desire in your heart. Don't trade your authenticity for trying to squeeze to fit in.

There is a point inside of you in your heart where you feel literally that you tired, things have been deplorable. You have been going on suffering forever. This the point of destruction in you where you are going on taking actions from a place of being you are not good enough, you deserve to suffer, life is all about suffering, you deserve to be punished, you are not liked, you are not loved , you are not important enough. It's this point where you are being destructive to your own life believing that you need to or have to suffer because you have not seen a life devoid of suffering. You think you have to suffer because there's no other way out. This is also the point of creation of your life from where you are creating a reality where you are suffering more and more. Each point of resistance is a place which is creating a shield to not receive love in the chest space. Just understanding that the shield created is from the programming of limiting beliefs will drop it and cause a shift at the core.

You may feel you are not worthy of it, you may feel you don't deserve it, you may feel like you are not good enough. In this state you may feel that you deserve to go through what you are enduring. You may feel like life is but an extension of suffering. You may feel like your birth was merely an error. You may feel like all bad things happen especially to you. You may feel like you were born unlucky. You may feel like you do want to give up. You may feel like you don't want to live anymore. You may feel like this pain is terrible and no one deserves to go through this. You may feel like enough is enough and is there no way out of it?

You may feel like life is happening to you and not for you. You may feel like no one loves you. You may feel like suffering is the only reality of your life. You may feel like you really want a way out of this.

The way out is a realisation that you suffering and feeling so much torture and pain because you are choosing to feel that way. You are choosing to suffer. You are choosing to feel the pain. You are choosing to be in that state. But you can choose not to suffer . You can choose to come out of there. You can choose to end the long term affair that you have with suffering . You can choose to cut all ties with suffering. You can choose not to feel dreadful anymore. Even though you feel, it's not your choice but you feel so dreadful that you are helpless. You have no other option but to suffer. But that's also a choice. You can choose to force yourself to feel good by believing that you can have your manifestation if you can create that pressure by feeling good – it alone will create a humongous breakthrough. Change the meaning you assign to your feeling to shift that feeling to a preferred feeling

No matter what happened till now that which puts you here, in this condition. In this very state in your heart you can choose not to experience suffering anymore. You can choose not to feel so terrible. You can choose to feel better now. You can choose to feel like you deserve to be happy. You can choose to receive the love. You can choose to forgive yourself. You can choose to give yourself a second chance. You can choose to not punish yourself anymore. You can choose not to destroy your happiness anymore by feeling that blistering pain. You can choose to feel so good and loved that the penetrating agony of the blister stops pressing you from within. You may now choose to not put yourself in more tests & karma.

You may now let go of the destructive emotions oozing out from the point of destruction in you. You can choose to stop hurting. You can choose to not cultivate reasons to suffer. You can choose to believe at the core of your being that now things should work out for you, you deserve things to work out for you. You deserve to receive all the joy. You deserve to receive all the breakthrough. You deserve to get absolutely lucky at the core. You deserve to get so lucky that only all good things happen to you and your loved ones. You deserve to feel so blessed that in every part of your being blessings are received. You deserve to be so loved that your partner is going out of their way to show up for you. You deserve to receive so much love that love is penetrating through your very being. You deserve justice so much that justice is penetrating through your being. You deserve to feel this love so much that this love is filling in every corner of your being. You deserve a miracle so much that this miracle is infused and imbibed in your being. You deserve to get so lucky that extreme luck is penetrating to your being. You deserve so much surprises, gifts and prizes that recognition, surprises, gifts, acknowledgement and prizes are penetrating through your being. You deserve to get so lucky that you are breaking free from the tangles of pain you were in for years and are experiencing a reality that proves it to you everyday that you just can get lucky. You deserve so much permanence in good luck and miracles that every day in every way you experience miracles. You deserve to be forgiven and loved so much that you are receiving consolation prize of support for all the pain you have endured, from the angels now as a confirmation you are being informed that you are completely forgiven now. You deserve to be chosen so much now that you are being chosen by all. You deserve to be nurtured so much now that your person is being nurturing and caring towards you. You deserve the exact kind of love that you desire from your partner so much that your partner is giving you that. You deserve God so much that God's love is penetrating through your heart. You deserve support, blessings, love, abundance, healing and miracles so much that all of them are infusing in one to become all that you are. You are healed. You have received your manifestation

A lot of us suffer and ruin our lives feeling like we are responsible for how others feel and in that course we affect our own personal boundaries. You are not here to please the whole world. It's not your responsibility how someone else is feeling when you are choosing your personal boundaries. You don't have to be a good person and you don't have to feel guilty for not choosing to be a good person. Being a good person doesn't mean violation of personal boundaries. You don't have to make others feel good at the cost of bleeding within. You don't have to do it because it looks good on the outside in a so called civilised society. You don't have to feel bad for living life on your own terms. You don't have to feel bad for choosing to create an ideal reality of your own. You don't have to feel bad for putting yourself first. You don't have to feel painful for choosing to love yourself. You don't have to be in a state where you question whether a decision is right or wrong. "There is nothing either good or bad, but thinking makes it so."- William Shakespeare.

You don't have to think in the way which makes you feel like the victim of the past or present but instead you can now think in a way where you are thinking to not choose to be a victim of your circumstances anymore. But you are thinking rather of overcoming these inner barriers and so are thinking of being someone who gets what they want. You are thinking that you don't have to feel bad. You are thinking that no one will punish you. But you are thinking that you are accepted just as you are and also are thinking that what you want ,your partner too wants that.

Choose your truly authentic being version – that's your best version you can choose to be, first and foremost you will feel happy from within and secondly being you unapologetically , attracts the rest smoothly . I can serve God anyway. I don't need a twin flame to feel more connected to God. It's my absolute belief. However this book I believe will get me closer to the exact kind of lover I've always looked for. It's my self concept that this book is going to get you back your person , exactly how you desire.

Don't reach out to them, don't stalk them when you are in desperation and needy state. Stop associating to what the past was like. I understand it was "trash." Now the current reality is more terrible and makes you feel powerless. So now we know where you stand. Now comes the moment when you shall go on a journey of self concept with me. This will take you to state where you have stopped affirming things like they are a playboy, instead you believe they love you a lot, it's possible for them to give you the kind of commitment that you desire. They are realising they too truly need the kind of love that you need. In other words your relationship attachment style is a perfect fit for each other, you both of syncing in here, at this level. Let's dive deep now into the core beliefs and your self concept, to take you to a state where you can know your manifestation into being.

To begin with the vast topic that this is in itself - core beliefs. Here are three statements where I have changed the core beliefs for an exemplary purpose, which will help you to understand this process better as we proceed further now to understand core beliefs on a deeper note.

Limited Belief : The manifestation won't happen. Way to Shift: I am always manifesting. The idea that manifestation won't happen that itself is a manifestation. So since words create thoughts and thoughts generate feelings and emotions, I choose to believe manifestation is real and I'm on this journey. It's a process which I now choose to trust.

Limited Belief : My partner has moved on. Way to Shift : I'm in a relationship with my partner already. The idea my partner has moved on is itself a manifestation in itself. So since I create my reality by thoughts, feelings and emotions, I choose to feel and believe that my partner hasn't moved on and we are now in a relationship already. Thank you God.

Limited Belief : But it will not work out for me. Way to Shift : It has already worked out for me. I know that it will not work out for me is a manifestation in itself so I choose to believe , feel and know that it has completely worked out for me . I'm in the desired relationship with my partner. Thank you God.

Disclaimer: You cannot change something or someone on the outside but you can change your idea of the thought and feeling of how you think and feel they are feeling about you at each point in time. When you change how you perceive and receive that how they feel about you, they too change their feeling about you. This is applicable for anyone and everyone in your reality. People can subconsciously hear you. When you meet a person and develop a certain understanding as in what they are thinking / feeling about you or something or someone else– by changing that assumption and feeling about you/situation/someone - how you want them to feel, you can make them feel/think exactly how you want them to feel /think. I am talking to you at the centre of your heart, in your chest space, where you constantly are suffering. You are suffering because you believe that you have to suffer. You think you cannot feel the way how you used to feel unless they come back. However you have to first feel that feeling and act if it's real to manifest it. It's safe to believe you are so powerful and life can be this magical. Nothing is right. Nothing is wrong. It's just perspective of humans like you and I. So many religion, so many God, they all point inwards. The power all along has been within. The feeling that you are feeling now is your state of consciousness currently, consciousness is your perspective, it is from what, where & how you understand everything now(at this very moment/ at every given point of time). We are always seeing the current reality through the vibration of our current core understanding. When we realise more and our wisdom gets inculcated- we experience a sense of shift within, a rise in core our frequency & vibration

Understanding- What did you understand now when you are reminded that your exact manifestation is here? How grateful are you to God? Just by believing we can manifest. This is how really seriously powerful manifestation is and God is. How much humble do you feel now? How much can you really believe? What are your questions? What's your current state of understanding?

Knowing- Understanding that it's possible and knowing nothing is right or wrong but you can have your partner exactly how you desire in your feelings - furthermore without attaching to the idea whether they will show up or not, letting go of the desire for them to show up. Know they have already shown up now. That's faith. Inculcate that

Being – You are being the person who has received your exact manifestation. Remember to check in – in your heart /chest space where you feel essence of your being and dare to be the one who has received their manifestation.

First you feel, then know and finally believe then the manifestation appears. This is the secret

Nothing terrible will happen right? It'll not. It'll all be in your favour! Just something won't go wrong where everything is against me right? No it'll all be in your favour. Something terrible will not happen that breaks my heart into pieces again right? No they won't. Things exactly will be according to the way I desire right? Yes things exactly will be how you desire. Nothing will go wrong, right? Right nothing will go wrong. I am safe right? Yes you are safe.

My ex will come back right? Yes right your ex will come back. I will get that lucky , right? Yes you will get that lucky! Everything will work out and my ex will show up out of nowhere? Yes everything will work out and your ex will show up out of nowhere. My ex still loves me right? Yes your ex still loves you a lot. My ex has completely shown up right? Yes your ex has completely shown up. I am getting that lucky right? Yes you are getting that lucky? I am this blessed right? Yes you are this blessed. Life can be this peaceful right ? Yes life can be this peaceful. True lovers really unite right? Yes true lovers really unite. I am safe to manifest right? Yes I'm safe to manifest. No ghost or black magic is involved right? Nothing harmful is induced. I am completely protected to create my own reality right? I am completely protected to create my own reality. I have manifested my desire, exactly how I desire right? Yes I have manifested my desire exactly how I desire

Remember nothing is off limits. Everything is possible and nothing is impossible. If you think you can't have what you desire then that'll manifest. If you believe you can then you will manifest that. You can choose anything. You decide what is good for you and what is bad for you, not society, not this is how it's, not standard, not your ex, not your in laws, not any spiritual guru, not anyone else. You decide what works for you and what doesn't. In your reality you decide what's right, what's wrong. What's true for you may not be true for another and that doesn't mean anyone is wrong here. Something might be a right decision for you, the same might be a wrong choice for another. It's right for you because after taking that decision, it goes in your favour. It's wrong for you when taking that decision lead to something that doesn't feel good to you or is a loss or is not in your favour. You create your reality. If you think your ex can come back exactly the way you desire and it's possible. They will.

You have to let go of the current reality. Accept that the current reality is a vibration and by changing the frequency you can change it to how you prefer it to be . Just choose that the current vibration is shifting wholly to the new frequency in which you want it to vibe in . The choice has to come from a strong belief where you are convinced that by choosing this, miracle can happen. Therefore choose to be the frequency of yourself who has it all in their best interest exactly how they choose and determine their best interest to be

"Imagining the Preferred Result"

We are going to imagine your ex preparing to send you a message, or to call you or to ping you on a social media .

You can imagine one of them, or all of them and as many times as you want. But, the best thing about this exercise is that you will pretend as if watching them do this. Visualization or scripting will work, even doing both simultaneously will. So, choose what you feel drawn to and come up with a scenery where your ex is writing a text to you. Imagine them struggling to find the right word. Imagine them carefully chalking out what they really want to tell you, in a note pad to get a favourable response from you. You can even imagine your person really tensed and anxious. It doesn't matter if you don't know what phone model your specific person currently has, just imagine the glimpse you can get or the vive of the situation.

For receiving a call, imagine them hearing the phone ringing and their heart palpitate to now hear your voice! For the social media example, imagine your ex sending you a message on the messenger of your social media or replying in regards to a reply to your story. I want you to really feel proud about the importance your ex gives to all of these activities. They want to get it just right, and don't want to hurt you again. You can even imagine that you are not responding right away. Meanwhile they are losing sleep over it and checking their phone all the time.

Rewrite your story

You may think you have no control over what your ex think and does. However, you are constantly making an assumption in your mind about what you "think" your specific ex "thinks" about and this is extremely important when you think how they feel about you . The judgements you make in your world become truths in your tomorrows. It's up to you to empower your belief system in order to attract the kind of communication you desire. This is what as a coach I specialise in, changing your core beliefs. The key is to see the possibility, unless you see a possibility, you cannot manifest that.

It's time to stop imagining your specific person ignoring you, or having nothing to do with you. For example, if you have sent many texts to your specific person already without any response, how did you imagine them? Did you imagine them replying to your messages or deleting them? Did you imagine your person off with someone else who they prefer? Did you imagine your ex having no time for you, not caring about your feelings and being just mean to you?

Well, it's time to tell a new story because your new story will become your new reality. It's time to start considering new ideas into what can be, instead of supporting the current reality of lack that you see around. Till today what you were thinking your current reality is a reflection of that. For example, you could start imagining your ex is being drawn to you and wanting to talk to you. Now, you may be thinking that if this was true, then they wouldn't be ignoring you right now. But, ask yourself this... do you want to continue to attract more of the moment of lack that you are experiencing forever now or choose the breakthrough into the abundant world of having your desire exactly as you desire ? So, which state of being will get you there?

"You need to take the first steps. It's up to you to say "What if my ex as thinking about me right now, feeling bad that they could not reciprocate to my messages prior to this". That feels much better, right?. We need to stop focusing at the current moment or what's visible in the current physical reality and start creating a fresh new beginning.

Maybe your ex wasn't ignoring you. Maybe they were planning to text very soon. Maybe they missed the texts due to a technical error. Maybe they lost their phone. Those are all possibilities that don't put you in the mode of a sufferer and are also empowering. Most of all, your awareness of how you think your ex "thinks" about you is important to your success. So, let's imagine your ex imagining you. What do they see? Try to invent positive aspects of what you want to come. For example, this idea of your ex wanting to spend more time with you, having a married life with you , feeling like you are their ideal partner, one and only etc. Imagine your ex reading this book for the purpose of manifesting you! Wouldn't that be an amazing thought?

I want you to do a visualization or scripting where you pretend to believe in a story where your ex really needs you so much, that they are trying to manifest you and trying to attract you back. Imagine your specific person appreciating things about you and planning to make you the happiest person in the world. We need to start imagining your specific person as actually wanting the same things as you, instead of imagining they want something completely different.

This is when the communication opens up. This is when your specific person finally responds to those texts you sent and says words you have been waiting to hear.

I dedicate this book to God , to Jesus .This book is further dedicated to every true lover out there yearning to reconcile with the love of their life. True love always wins. Thank you God. Thank You Jesus. Thank You Mother Gaia. Thank You Angels.

You need to love the feeling of having it vibrationally, not be desperate of how it looks like on the physical reality. Without trying to get it but letting go & loving the feeling of having it, you'll actually end up being a match to it.

When you are manifesting a specific person, it's important to focus on the feeling of togetherness.

"Live your life in a sublime spirit of confidence and determination; disregard appearances, conditions, in fact all evidence of your senses that deny the fulfilment of your desire. Rest in the assumption that you are already what you want to be." -The Power of Awareness.

"I hope even 1% things will not go wrong." Remember this is a limiting belief

"I hope karma will not bite me." This is another limiting belief

"Even a little thing will not go wrong right?" -It's another limiting belief

I have nothing to fear right? There you go it's another limiting belief . You can now change the belief to you don't need to be afraid of fear of anything . Nothing outside of you has power until you feel afraid in your heart. When you feel afraid in your heart, remind yourself that it's safe to create the reality that you desire in your heart & you will be freed from the fear. The power is in the centre of your heart, relax and be what you feel now to understand where you are, on the inside. Don't be afraid of any resistance that you literally can feel, they are all limiting beliefs, in the light of God shining through you from within , you can uproot all the resistances from the core infusing in the powerful light you see and feel flowing as the very strength of your being . In that light of God you can teleport now in the frequency of light where you desire to go. Choose to feel how it feels to reach the destination of your desire in your heart , that's when you start to radiate the frequency to align to the absolute state of authenticity at the core of your being . This is how you quantum leap in the quantum field.

Having to let go of everything focus on why you desire what you desire and what is it that your values are, your desire are & that which you desire shall be fulfilled- focusing on that which you desire you'll be truly free and receive absolute clarity when you'll be able to truly relax from within- you will literally feel like it's done and in the event of being ready for your manifestation- you allow the magical portal to open , the thinning of the veil will happen for you and you and your partner will choose each other as one

Nothing else will go wrong in this process right? Choose to believe now it is all going right and in your favour from now onwards

No one will be harmed ? I won't die right? It's your limiting belief here again haunting you down . You are safe . No one is getting harmed in the process and you won't die . You will live a long, fruitful & healthy life aligned to your true authenticity. You are having a rebirth & awakening now. You are waking up to become the most free version of yourself , inside & out. You are becoming exactly who you prefer to be, the most.

No one will harm me right? You are completely protected and with God you are manifesting now & all the time . You are never alone

I am absolutely safe right? You are absolutely safe , chosen and protected

I don't have to choose for anyone else right? I can exactly manifest the person that I desire? Your true happiness is in the manifestation of your true desires. No matter what other supplements you seek for or in what ways you try to compensate or compromise for your desires, true happiness and joy is in allowing yourself to receive the exact manifestation that you desire . You don't have to settle for less or live by compromising to look good to others / for people who you don't even know.

You are the one who is allowing their manifestation to show up now

Whether someone is your twin flame or soulmate is not the issue but whether you feel that intense love for them at the core of your heart, that must be your concern . If you don't drop the labels, they are again limiting beliefs. Your twin flame or soulmate or love of your life is the one for whom your heart yearns now and if you have met them and are going through a terrible heartbreak from a break up that's from where you are reading this book .If you are single and don't have anyone to focus on, but feel like reconciling with an ex, even then this book is perfect for you . Focus on exactly what kind of relationship you desire with your ex, feel that into being, the rest shall line up for you, in absolute divine favour.

However if you are seeking for your specific person, still drop the desire , expectations , pain, idea of possible , impossible, right, wrong, holy , unholy, correct, incorrect, accepted , non accepted, chosen , non chosen , popular, unpopular, money making, not money making, fame giving, not fame giving , good for your future, not good for your future, looks good on the outside to look like a good or civilised person accepted by the society , doesn't look good on the outside or isn't accepted by society as a civilised choice & etc.

Beyond these limiting beliefs is another belief that none of these matter because your partner is aligning to the same perspective as yours and by virtue of the determination , you now feel the strength coming from the idea of their very presence in this version - feel the strength of your true power of authenticity , beyond who will think what, who will understand or not - by the virtue of choice of exploring the most magnificent - you are now choosing to live the life that you always desired and are thus allowing it to manifest in the outer realm/physical reality as well, your partner and everything is aligning in your favour to manifest what & how you have exactly desired it all to be - all your life with your heart and soul . Thank you God. So it's. Thus it shall be. Amen.

You have manifested the exact desire. You don't offend God if you don't please people but everything that you have known is someone else's point of view. In fact The Bible talks about praising the Lord & not being a people pleaser. Choose every action from a place of you are doing it for the love that you feel in your heart , you'll experience magnificent quantum leaps happening in each aspect of your life . You have to learn to not be comfortable to with your suffering to truly gear the determination to change things for you in your favour. Law of assumptions have helped me really with that.

You were just your own allowance and permission away .Now you are giving yourself the permission to have all that you desire and choose it all to be absolutely in your favour

You have received the call today . Your specific person has confirmed now for you in your immediate physical reality- you are now with the love of your life. You are in that relationship already that you always desired. Relax , let go and know it's done

You are the one who just allowed their true love to show up for them in the exact way that they desire.

You are the one who is now in a committed relationship with the love of their life

You are finally giving yourself the permission to believe that the exact way you desire , in that way your manifestation is showing up for you . Even though you have many options but still it's a choice by the virtue of which you are choosing this union at the core of your being now.

You are free now at the core of your being to fully give yourself the permission to experience this love, to call upon this manifestation to confirm and to allow yourself what you would feel when you finally have received your manifestation. You have received your exact manifestation now and you are giving yourself the permission in each corner of your being to receive this love now

You are experiencing a magnificent breakthrough now at the core of your being

You are free now in this allowance. You have given yourself the permission at the core and you are now taking the responsibility to unify with the love of your life at the core - and in that unification you are becoming one with your true love , your one true soul's mate , the love of your life - the extension of your being , the ultimate soulmate.

At the very core you had this breakthrough now, this shift where you have completely harmonised in oneness with the love of your life. You have had your breakthrough now. You have received all the permission to come into allowance to shift the game to receive this manifestation now

Your partner has now chosen you in the exact way you desire

Dropping everything else , every other path I choose to commit to the path that unifies me and my specific person. I cannot serve two masters so thanking everyone all across the globe I cut cords with the collective consciousness and unplug from what's happening now and choose to commit to the path of union with the love of my life now . I detach from what no longer serves me to only align to what is meant for my highest good. I choose this harmonious union now very specifically in the way I desire with the person I wish to be with. I drop all the how it will happen and now believe that it has happened now for me . Exactly the way I desire in that exact way the love of my life has shown up for me . Fearlessly you can let go of the grip now . You can now break free from everything and can fly in joy of really knowing that manifestation is magical. Every blockage is casting itself away saluting the intensity of your love and you are now literally seeing your higher self. You are now moving past many barriers , you have finally geared up all the strength to drop all the resistances. As God embraces and loves you , you feel at the core something really is moving and as you keep gearing up this momentum fearlessly in the centre of your chest - you experience a magnificent breakthrough where at the core of your being every burden is now being dropped. Eventually you are letting all parts of your triggers - holding you back go . At the core you are finally cracking up to shine like the diamond that you are

Universe Is Showering Wonderful Relationships In My Life! I Am Healthy And Happy In My Life!

You are experiencing back to back shifts everyday . Miracles are a part of your life. You are now experiencing all the good things in your life . Finally you are in the state of alignment. Every barricade has fallen away and at the core the flip has happened, you have aligned to become who you truly are /who you prefer to be. You remember where it all began and your true soul calling is getting more clear to you- you are here now, walking the most holistic path of manifesting who you love at the very core essence of your being. It'll all lead to them manifesting in your life. Don't be afraid to let go . Your desire is deep seated in you . Your manifestation is yours it can never be taken away from you . You have got this

Luck can come to me too? I also can get lucky? Luck can favour me too? I can also have a breakthrough? Breakthroughs and miracles really happen? Miracle is really real? People actually experience this kind of blessing filled miracle for real? I'm seriously one of those people who is receiving this kind of success? I am the person who believes it's possible for miracles to exist. Miracle can really happen to me? I can be the one to get so lucky to experience miracles? Yes I can get this lucky that I can experience any kind of miracle? I can receive this love and this love will not be taken away from me? I can also be successful?

Success is really real? One fine day the inner work does lead to success? I can also be successful? I can have success too? I can actually be successful? People can really get successful? I can receive the success seriously?

Seriously breakthrough is real and I just had a breakthrough?

In this section, I will help you to look at the blocks that you might have to getting love.

Love Block 1: Questioning your ex's point of view

Not trusting or feeling like they have an hidden agenda when they are loving you or feeling like that change will not be permanent

You always question their agenda, you are complaining about the past. You are complaining about their current behaviour.

You complain about their choices and everything that they are choosing. You are feeling like that's what they want and that's further making you feel helpless about the situation

You are stuck over what they have said, how things look like, what they are saying or choosing now. You think this is how it's going to be

This is the perpetual cycle of thought pattern holding you back from releasing this block

Love Block 2: Feeling despicable

You may feel you are not worthy of receiving the love that you seek from your ex

You don't love yourself enough or feel like a victim of your circumstances. You might also have deserving issues

You might be feeling like you deserve to be punished for some fault of yours and thus are choosing to bleed because you think you need to sacrifice for love or you torture yourself.

You think what you seek is so horrendous that in no way your ex will give it to you. You are not embracing your uniqueness here. Somewhere you are ashamed of who you are, you need choose to let of the feeling bad feeling and even the idea that guilt equals to feeling bad & forgive it at the core. When you do so , this block shall be lifted.

Love Block 3: We accept that we don't justify it

You accept other people's point of view as verdict and feel like you are a victim to your circumstances

You hear something and immediately react or feel hopeless. You feel like you cannot change anything about the situation but that's it. This is when you still believe that something outside has power over you

You think how other people perceive things is the ultimatum but that's just another interesting point of view

Love Block 4: Reliant upon correspondence

You adhere to what is and feel like the outside circumstances have power over you

You may even feel that it's in the hand of destiny and let your current resonance create your reality

You feel powerless, scared and continue to give your power away, still trying to connect the dots, much overwhelmed.

Everything is connected, it's happening in perfect order. Everyone has free will and with your free will you have strength to choose how you want your reality to be. In your reality, it's about giving power only to your free will & living life for yourself, in your favour, as per your preference.

Love Block 5: Fear of disaster

You focus on the worst possible scenario and what can go wrong than what can go right

You get extremely pessimistic to focus on the worst case scenario

A great way you get over these blocks is chakra healing. Here are some affirmations for the same

You can only think of what can go wrong because you cannot even expect your ex to come back. So choose what can go right and try to expect, once you have geared the strength to expect, you'll be with your ex.

Affirmations for every chakra :

Root Chakra: I feel safe and connected to mother earth.

Sacral Chakra: I am creative; I forgive the past and embrace the present moments.

Solar Plexus Chakra: I am the blessed child of God ; I have the power to express myself.

Heart Chakra: I am open for love and I love unconditionally.

Throat Chakra: I clearly express my thoughts and I speak what is true.

Third-Eye Chakra: I am developing divine and intuitive insight.

Crown Chakra: I feel connected with other beings, with heaven and earth, the whole

Core Belief Transition Chart – The Most Important Step

Before You Explore Affirmations

When In Extremely Fearful State :

1. It is not possible my partner is showing up. It has been possible and my partner has shown up

2. It's impossible that just by words we can create our reality. It's possible that just by words we create our reality . At first there was words and words became thoughts.

3. It's impossible my partner still loves me? It's possible my partner still loves me

4. After all that happened it's impossible for us to unite? After all that had happened it was still possible for us to reunite & we reunited

5. Even if we get back things cannot be the way I want. Even though I thought so but now upon reconciling I see it's exactly the way I wanted and it therefore has always been, is and will always be possible to manifest anything exactly the way I desire – just by believing it's really possible

6. I am not being chosen. I have already been chosen. I am the chosen one in my reality. My partner loves me a lot.

7. I don't think miracles really happen. Miracles have happened for me and I am experiencing them all the time in my life

8. God is never there for me. God has always been there for me

9. I will get hurt ultimately if I have the hope that they will come back. My hope lead to faith and it's the belief of a resilient being that creates the momentum to break through the resistances to believe at core of the being that it has manifested now & that's how manifestations shows up in the pressure that these emotions create – that momentum manifests

10. But for me it will not work. But for me it has worked now and I already have my result

11. My partner hasn't shown up yet. My partner has shown up now

12. My partner at the core of their heart is not in my team. My partner at the core of their heart is in my team

13. My partner doesn't seek the kind of commitment that I seek.. My partner seeks the exact kind of commitment that I seek

When In A State Of Confusion But Hopeful:

1. I can't believe this kind of magic can happen with me , for me, in my life. This kind of magic has happened for me in my life

2. I can't believe a human being can be this blessed. I am that human being who has all along been this blessed. I am realising my worth now in Lord

3. I didn't know God is this real. God is really this real

4. I can't believe this relationship is possible. We have already reconciled

5. I can't imagine I had so much of resistances inside. I am now free off these resistances

6. I can't really feel my true potential. I now feel my true potential

7. I can't understand my true worth. I now feel my true worth

8. I can't really be at ease. I am now at ease

When finally feeling good , you can believe that your partner can come, you are feeling happy :

1. I can't believe this relationship is really meant to happen. This relationship has happened already. It all has worked out for me

2. I can't believe after all these we could reconcile. We have reconciled already exactly in the way how I desire. I'm that blessed . I can relax at the core of my soul

3. I can't believe I can get that lucky and blessed. I understand God is truly real & great and thus I can be truly lucky and blessed

4. I didn't know human beings have so much power in them. Now I know and literally feel in my heart that I am so powerful

5. I didn't know my heart chakra could open again. My heart chakra has opened now

6. I can't believe I am so chosen. I am this chosen. I have always been chosen. I am the chosen one. I am being chosen at the core of my very being now

7. I can't believe life is so magical. Life is extremely magical

8. I can't believe life is so literally real. Life is so literally real

9. I can't believe I have been accepted as how I am by my partner. My partner has accepted me exactly how I desire

10. My partner seriously will come back for me? My partner has come back for me

11. My partner really loves me? My partner really loves me and chooses me at the core of their being

12. Manifestation really works? Yes manifestation is real

13. My partner actually loves ME? Yes my partner actually love me.

14. My partner is actually in my team?Yes my partner is actually in my team

15. It has all finally worked out for me? It has all really worked out for me

16. My partner is choosing me at the core? Yes my partner has chosen me at the core

17. My exact manifestation is actually here? I am actually in a relationship with my partner once again

18. My partner has really chosen me? My partner is absolutely always there for me

19. My partner is the one for me? It has all worked out with my partner

20. God really loves us? God is really choosing us

21. God really loves me? God knows that I exist

22. I am actually visible to God, God really knows that I exist? God really is real

23. God is always there for me? God is always choosing me

24. I am the one who is now experiencing a breakthrough? I can be both the masterpiece and work in progress simultaneously

25. I am here now? I have received my exact manifestation how I always wanted

26. It was really possible to have it all? Life is that magnificent

27. In God really all things are possible? Impossible is nothing

28. God really does magic? The magic really happened

29. I for the first time can truly relax and trust that manifestation is here? Now it makes sense

30. The miracle really happened for me? The universe did conspire in my favour

31. Life definitely is not happening to me ? Life is happening for me

32. Universe really loves me?I am really chosen and favoured by the universe

33. God loves me beyond measure? I can feel the presence of God

34. God always sends me signs? I'm filled in with signs from heaven

35. God is always there for me?I really have nothing to fear

36. Every fear is another limited belief? Fear is just a limited conditioning and I choose it to not be real

37. The love that I seek in that love now I'm one? I am in a relationship and it was all possible. Life is this good & amazing

38. The entire universe really conspired for us to reunite? True love does win. It was all happening to make me understand truly what I deeply seek at the core existence of my being

39. I deserve this love. I deserve this second chance? This is my true soul calling, this is the true extension of my being.

40. I deserve to receive all the love and respect for the worth of my magnificence? I am respected , adored and appreciated beyond measure

41. God forgives all sin. I am forgiven from the core of my being? I am loved in each corner of my existence and I'm acknowledged

42. God holds no grudge. I forgive my partner completely and allow the aspect of my partner in me to forgive me now fully and this really works? I can forgive, to forgive I don't have to be a saint. I can just relax and choose to forgive at the core of my being and let go now

43. Nothing that I experience will trigger me again I forgive the sensation of triggers. Just by choosing I can really release it all? We are that lucky emotionally in the core of our heart – just by making a choice to feel better because we deserve it, just by acknowledging it we can choose to feel better. Nothing is right or wrong. We can choose to do, be, feel anything. The association of the pain that something is wrong, in that core space - I just need to know that which I perceive as wrong is not wrong. Everything is a perspective. So I can choose to feel

good knowing it's not wrong. You will not be punished and humiliated for your choice. You can choose not to feel humiliated . So you are appreciated for being absolutely right in your universe – by the essence of your very being. This is why you feel relaxed as you can let go of it all and know, believe and feel it's done. Miracle has happened. It's a choice. You have chosen the miracle to happen by creating the safe haven within by believing you deserve it and it's possible. Now you are in alignment, so you have your exact manifestation magically. Anyone can choose anything. We're free beings. We are free to choose to feel, do and be anything at any point of time

44. I am loved at the core of my being. Life is really real. I can relax now fully and choose to know that everything we know is someone's perspective so when we focus on perspective, we create our own reality, we create our own universe, we create our own miracles- consciously

Core Wounds & Core Insecurities Clearing

I can't believe I will receive the exact kind of commitment that I desire. I have received the exact kind of commitment that I desire

My partner will trigger my insecurities and try to fix me. My partner accepts me in my core insecurities and make me feel comfortable and relaxed there. My partner doesn't choose the kind of commitment that I choose deep down. My partner has chosen the kind of commitment that I have chosen deep down

My partner doesn't really desire me on their own. My case is different. It's exceptionally a tough and painful one. My partner desires me on their own and easily and effortlessly I now have manifested my desire. It was this easy My partner makes me feel relaxed at the core of the essence of my being. And I choose to feel more of this sensation now

I feel calm and composed in my partner's presence and I choose to relax, feel and know that

I am in a state of alignment now. I feel extremely relaxed

I am filled with abundance of blessings now

The difficult times are over for me . I can relax in absolute harmony

I am ready for the absolutely new beginning in our relationship with the desired partner of my choice – in the exact version I desire. I am in a relationship already and it is getting better and better every passing day. I have experienced the unexpected miracle

If you have noticed this book has a lot of numbers as well. Each time you randomly open the book as an oracle, also try to feel what meaning and message you are interpreting from your heart space for the number mentioned on that page. You can also look up on the internet, the message you receive in coherence to your search of that number and that which you are then most drawn to is the message for you. God is always communicating with all of us through the universe. We are all one in God. The feeling you feel in your heart space, always makes you feel a certain way and that is an indicator of where you are now.

In that place in your heart integrate the understanding that it's all possible. Miracles really happen. All these things are really possible . Your exact desired manifestation has shown up for you exactly the way you desire. Life is a magical miraculous joy full of blessings, ease and joy. God is the magic. You have the resistances as long as you feel them, the moment you choose not to feel them, you can replace them. Just with the new belief that all resistances are gone and you have received exactly that what you seek will push out to manifest that for you. Know your manifestation into existence.

Just know your manifestation is done. Just know your ex has already shown up. Just know every affirmation that you are about to read are true and know your ex is already here. Know that you have the perfect health, life, wealth, friends, community, love, relationship, support, finances and spiritual well being, in absolutely harmony as you truly desire it to be now. Know you have it all. Know you have manifested the exact version of your ideal reality. It's done.

Stage 1 : I want it now

1. I call in the serene odes of breezes and flowers to me kissing me now – taking me beyond the presence of my being, everything else falls apart all along it was just us.

2. Tulips, roses, orchids maroon, mingled in shinning golden, I have found my soul moulded in yours

3. Colours sprinkle, daffodils shine, you and I have found us fine

4. Possible impossible thousand worries beyond them you and I are the poets

5. Pondered here , pondered there I find my home in your heart sphere

6. Sing songs of love and more, find me in a magic spur

7. Towards the end I rise in your shinning light

8. Here there everywhere it's all about our affair

9. Intoxicated and forlorn it always lead back to you my love

10. Nothing apart from you I think of and in the song of ecstasy we tune in now in absolute oneness & serendipity

Stage 2 : Is there a way?

1. I have loved you in every way and I will love you in every way , shape and form

2. You are the core of my soul

3. You are an extension of my being

4. It's you and it has always been you

5. You are the love of my life

6. It all starts and ends with you

7. You meet me where I live within

8. You are the one I've always been looking for

9. In every way I was always looking for you

10. There's nothing that can ever take you away from the core of my being

Stage 3 : My heart is yearning for you

1. I love you and only you

2. I am the one you are craving for

3. I am the one you can't live without

4. It is all about me and you

5. You see me wherever you go

6. You are seeking me from every corner of your being

7. You miss me beyond the breadth of your soul

8. There is nobody you like to be with but me who has your soul

9. We're the same soul literally

10. Your heart & mine beat as one

Stage 4 : Make them obsessed

1. You ,you ,you and only you that's who I seek

2. In the deepest core of my existence you are persistent

3. You miss me beyond all the resistance

4. You are craving for me incessantly now

5. You can think of nothing but my existence

6. I mean the world to you

7. I am the love of your dreams

8. If you can think of anything then it's how it feels to be with me

9. You so want to touch me

10. Your life is all about me

Stage 4 : Get into their head

1. You love me and only me. It all along has been about me

2. You are choosing me above all

3. You feel home with me

4. You are choosing me because you love me

5. You are in my team because it's your choice

6. You share my perspective because it naturally makes you the most comfortable in your heart space

7. You feel good to be with me that's why you have chosen me above all

8. You trust me and your perspective is my perspective and it doesn't matter what others say

9. You always choose what am choosing

10. You are always synced in oneness with me

Stage 5 : Make them think of you

1. Everyone and everything reminds you of my presence

2. You feel me in every place - inside and outside

3. You cannot rest in any other reality

4. Only I feel real to you

5. I am the one and only in your reality

6. You see me in everything that your eyes go to

7. You are always sent signs from angels that are reminding you of me

8. You miss me even while eating food

9. Even things you overhear also sound like my voice to you

10. Every song you hear sounds like our song to you

Stage 6 : Make them acknowledge you

1. You finally took a stand for me

2. You finally have the courage to be in my team

3. You finally prioritised me above all

4. Finally once again as always I'm your first preference

5. You finally understood how much I really love you

6. I am the love of your every desire

7. I mean the world to you

8. You can't live without me

9. You are my best friend

10. I am your best friend

Stage 7 : Make them choose you now

1. You just called me

2. Finally your call came

3. Finally you chose to call me

4. Finally it feels so good to you for to you to call me

5. Finally you called me to give me the kind of commitment that I have asked for

6. Finally you have chosen me above all

7. Finally I have it all

8. I am the love you were always looking for

9. I mean the world to you

10. Your day starts and end with me

Stage 8 : Make them commit

1. You are so committed to me

2. All you can think of is me

3. Thank you for being so loyal to me

4. We have loyal hearts

5. 5. I love you

6. Everything is perfect

7. I can trust the process

8. I feel so safe in this space

9. Everything now is so literally true

10. I can feel the magic of manifestation

Stage 9 : Marriage Manifestation

1. We finally got married..

2. Our marriage pictures have come so well

3. Life is amazing after marriage

4. We have been to so many trips ever since we got married

5. Our honeymoon was beautiful

6. I am so loved by my partner

7. My partner always makes me feel special

8. I am my partner's favourite person

9. My partner shares the same perspective as mine

10. My partner's family loves me a lot

Stage 10 : Living Together

1. We watch movies together

2. My partner takes interest in my interest

3. My partner and I are on the same page

4. My partner always tells me that all along he was looking for someone exactly just like me

5. My partner loves to spend time with me

6. I am the love of their life

7. My partner feels whole in my presence

8. I mean the world to my partner

9. My partner feels like we've known each other in past lives

10. My partner is married to my soul

Stage 11 : Love is real

1. Love united us

2. It was love that wanted to see us together once again

3. We are love's favourite choice

4. We are the love of love's life

5. Love is always choosing us

6. Love has chosen us to be together

7. We are love favoured

8. Love can't think of a better love as it's very own literal expression than ours

9. We are loved by each other

10. We are always loving each other

Stage 12 : It's all about love

1. Love is the writer of our story

2. Love is always bringing you closer to me

3. You have always loved me

4. I am loved by you extremely

5. You find me irresistibly hot

6. It's love's magic that always keeps you attracted to me..

7. Our story isn't over, it hasn't even started yet

8. God is the reason we prosper in delight everyday . Thank you God

9. I always make you happy

10. Every time that you hear the word love, you think of me

Stage 13 : Magic of love

1. You always make me feel so special

2. I am the fairy of your magical realm

3. I'm the one you were always looking for

4. You think of nothing but coming closer to me

5. I am the greatest blessing in your life

6. You always want to go out of your way to do things for me

7. I am that special to you

8. You can't take your eyes off me

9. You love to touch and feel my essence

10. I'm the art of the artist in you

Stage 14 : My heart beats for you

1. My heart loves you

2. My heart has always known you

3. Everything around the world is happening to bring us together

4. Everything in this universe wants to see us together

5. I am chosen one in your favour

6. I am the love you always desired

7. Every part of your cell is speaking to my cells

8. Each wound in you cries my name out , I'm the healer of your soul

9. My presence heals the existence of your being

10. I come to your dreams every night

Stage 15 : One heart

1.   We always feel the same thing

2.   We are always connected telepathically

3.   You love me beyond measure

4.   I am the chosen one in your universe

5.   I am the one and only one you desire

6.   You feel I meet you where you live

7.   Everything in your life starts with me

8.   I am your dream come true

9.   I mean the world to you

10. I am the one who makes you feel content and secure

Stage 16 : You are my life

1.   We are always choosing each other

2.   We can't think of a moment without each other

3.   We create a revolution in love together

4.   We are the children of God

5.   We are the rainbow warriors of Christ

6.   In God we unify

7.   God is uniting us

8.   God is in our team

9.   God favours our union

10. God loves to see us together

Stage 17 : You complete me

1. You are the one I'm in a relationship with

2. You are the one who is present in front of me now physically

3. You are the one I'm holding the hand of now

4. You are the one in my room, seated next to me

5. You are the one who is holding my heart

6. You are the one who I belong to

7. You are the one who took a stand for me

8. You are the one who is so protective of me

9. You are the one who is claiming me

10. You are the one who is always choosing me.

Stage 18 : I finally met you

1. You finally pushed out to be exactly me.

2. You are the exact reflection of who I am within

3. I feel perfect and comfortable to be who I wish to be with you

4. You instil in me the thrill to have my own doctrine of philosophy

5. We share the same idea of right and wrong

6. We are made for each other

7. We are created from the same essence

8. Our love is true and real

9. We are the human version of love personified

10. Our love creates all the magic in this world

Stage 19 : It feels so good to see you

1. I knew this will happen one day

2. You are very special to me

3. I like to look at you

4. I love how we just met where we are now

5. Our lives always have been parallel

6. We deep down are one & the same

7. I love the way you love me

8. Thank you for showing up in my reality

9. Finally we have reconciled now

10. I love that this union finally has happened

Stage 20 : I am ready to meet you

1. I am ready to receive your call now

2. I know truly it's possible that you'll call me today

3. I am so glad you are calling me now

4. We finally had a talk

5. I love the way you love me

6. I love the intensity with which you love me

7. I love how you are my ultimate breakthrough that makes me break free

8. I love that you changed the alignments of the stars to be with me

9. You are the ray of the light in my heart

10. You are my dream that just came true

Stage 21 : The break up happened for good

1. I love how we both agree it all happened for good

2. It was a journey across parallel realities and of gathering great knowledge and exploration

3. We are more transparent and now completely more raw to each other

4. We now share the ultimate togetherness we both were looking for

5. We have met in each other exactly where we fell apart within

6. No one knows us the way we know each other

7. We are what we were looking for

8. Our union was written in the stars even before we were born.

9. We are proud of each other

10. We often get nostalgic and relive the old times in our imagination

Stage 22 : I am your love

1. We never stopped loving each other

2. We were searching for each other all the time

3. We could imagine it is possible to reconcile & visions were creating themselves

4. We share the same frequency

5. We meet each other inside our hearts

6. Our heart beats in one feeling

7. We both are ready to love each other

8. We both are mesmerised in each other

9. We both feel safe with each other

10. We both are here for the same mission

Stage 23 : I am the magic

1. The magic is in me

2. Nothing outside of me has power over me

3. God is love

4. God favours those with pure conscience filled in with pure love

5. My partner is the reflection of the essence of my being

6. What I feel my partner feels the same

7. My partner loves me at the core of their heart

8. The whole world is celebrating our oneness now

9. My heart now sings the song of this euphony

10. My partner's soul sings in the same tune as mine

Stage 24 : We share the same soul

1. Symphony , rhythm, alliteration of poetry they were all being decorated for this moment of glory

2. Everything suddenly is aligning to unify for us

3. We were meant to meet my love

4. You meet me beyond my physical vessel

5. You meet me where I feel I am alive

6. We come from the same source

7. You are literally my other half

8. You accelerate my momentum of creation

9. You instil in me the best vibration

10. You are the greatest strength in an order of the heavenly perfection

Stage 25 : It was written in the stars

1. Out of nowhere God made it happen

2. Suddenly out of the blue you showed up

3. When I wasn't even expecting you showed up

4. I felt very calm and was doing something else altogether when you showed up

5. I thanked God that I trusted the process

6. Thank you Jesus that my wish came true

7. It was beyond the fear of my dreams shattering I dared to choose & now we're already together

8. It felt so good to act as if we were together already

9. Thank You Jesus for sending my partner in the exact version that I desire them in

10. We are so blessed to reunite

Stage 26 : Love is my name

1. I love the way we often remake our past memories & heal them together

2. I love how all our fetishes are exactly aligned as always

3. I love how you have always dared to take so many leap of faith for me

4. I love how our love has made me a better person

5. I love to smooch you

6. I just love when our lips meet

7. I love that you love me so much

8. I love that we equally missed each other

9. I love how our love has created a new history for tomorrow.

10. I love how you gape at me

Stage 27 : You meet me where I live

1. You are extremely delicious & juicy

2. You only want me

3. All along you were seeking for me

4. You are missing me now

5. You are letting go of all the resistances

6.   You are finally coming towards me

7.   You and I are literally one being at the core

8.   I am choosing to be with you now

9.   I am married to you

10. I am the one who is your child's other parent

Stage 30 : Love is eternal

1.   Not for a day did you stop loving me

2.   You love me and only me

3.   You are constantly thinking of me

4.   Beyond every barrier I'm the one who is your first choice

5.   I am the one who you prefer to be with

6.   I am the one who you feel the best with

7.   I am the one who makes you feel the best

8.   I am the one you feel at very centre of your heart

9.   I'm the one you have long forgiven

10. I am the one you forgive completely now

Stage 31 : Beyond the veil

1.   I am the one who is your perfect partner

2.   I am the one who you were always seeking for in everyone

3.   I am the one who makes you move the needle

4.   I am the one who makes you feel so young

5. I am the one who makes you want to do something new

6. I am the one who makes you drop everything to choose love

7. I am the one you love at the core most point of your existence

8. Since the beginning of our creation we were one

9. We meet each other in our most authentic state

10. We are exactly one and the same

Stage 32 : Chosen Ones

1. Our love for each other made us unique

2. Our love is deep and divine

3. This love is the love we've read about in literatures

4. Our love can heal every disorder

5. It is the idea our union that sets us free

6. We have unified fearlessly

7. My love for you in unconditional

8. I love you as an extension of my existence

9. You are a stretch of the light of my existence

10. Our love creates a new story that the world has never read

Stage 33 : The Exceptional

1. I love the way we are sexually compatible

2. We love to make love in the wildest way

3. Unified in the feeling of this love I can conquer every fear

4. The gift of being love just gives me all that I was ever seeking for

5. I'm committed to you

6. It's feels so good to be in a relationship with each other

7. We finally have the exact kind of relationship that we were always looking for

8. This feeling of union is the ultimate feeling of union with God

9. Our love is all that we needed ever

10. This love makes me feel like the ultimate winner

Stage 34:We are special

1. This is the love I always was looking for

2. This is the kind of relationship that I always wanted

3. This is the exact kind of partner I always wanted

4. God proved it that I can have it all

5. The love that I desire that finally has found me

6. The very way I always wanted to be loved I'm loved in that way

7. My partner is loving me in every possible way

8. My partner is choosing me always & their every choice is in the favour of our togetherness

9. I am the love of my partner's life

10. We finally had the ultimate breakthrough

Stage 35 : Thank you for choosing me

1. Thank you God for this moment of miracle

2. I can now feel how magic really happens

3. Thank you God for this grand opportunity

4. Thank you God for giving me an opportunity to serve you

5. Thank you God for this path

6. Thank you God for this love

7. Thank you God for reuniting us

8. Thank you God for giving me a chance to experience miracles in this lifetime

9. Thank you God for sending me this very love that I exactly asked for

10. Thank you God for giving me the strength, conviction, the power and determination to receive

Stage 36 : It is God's mercy

1. It's God's mercy that brought us back together again

2. We had to realize we were perfect anyway

3. Our true value is determined in God

4. Everything difficult has been released & has been lifted off our path

5. It doesn't matter how our union happens, this very feeling of unification is all that is I ever needed

6. At the core of my existence in God I'm choosing to commit to you now

7. I choose to always speak in the best of my own favour of interest

8. I choose to be completely be in my own team & absolute favor

9. I choose to take a stand for my own perspective. We belong to each other

10. I choose to acknowledge myself with the same respect I would acknowledge a fellow child of God with

Stage 37 : Because God promised

1. I put myself first now

2. It's in my conscience I feel satisfied to make this decision now that we are already together

3. I feel I deserve this gift of God

4. Love can do miracles

5. God is the power and strength I feel within

6. A magic is happening for me

7. This love has all along been with me

8. I'm in a relationship now

9. I feel so good to be in love with you

10. In every lifetime I'll choose to be with you

Stage 38 : When there's a will there's a way

1. I always was determined to be with you

2. It's my determination and conviction that makes me so resilient in love

3. Love is the point of creation

4. Something only gets destroyed for something better out of it to get recreated

5. I am blessed beyond measure

6. Every hurdle is being lifted from my path

7. I am receiving the greatest gift ever

8. The tables are turning in my favour

9. The puzzle pieces are matching

10. I was meant to do this

Stage 40 : I am yours my love

1. In my wildest desires I feel authentic to be rawly present with you

2. I can visualise myself absolutely naked with you

3. You make me feel safe like no one else

4. Our love always keeps me connected to the conscience

5. I strongly believed I'll get through this and we got through it

6. I truly intend from the core of my heart to be with you

7. I choose to believe we are already together now

8. I let go of the desire to be with you as I'm already with you

9. I dare to believe I'm with you now

10. I choose to know we are together right at this very moment and this was all along possible

Stage 41 : Forever one

1. God is real

2. God is the one in whom when we have faith we can achieve it all

3. In God we are unifying now

4. Faith is the new cool

5. I am a trend setter. We are the believers

6. True belief leads to magic

7. At the core I now believe that I already have my manifestation

8. I am chosen and favoured by God

9. This is God's plan

10. This is a part of the unfolding process

Stage 42 : It all makes sense

1. God loves us

2. God always fulfils his promises

3. God is always choosing us

4. Our desire comes from God

5. At the core of our hearts God is choosing us to be one

6. It's God's decree that we must be together now

7. God is writing a new story in our favour

8. We set our own new standards in the society now

9. We are the new ideal benchmark

10. We are the pioneer of the perspective of our life story

Stage 43 : Back to the roots

1. My partner and I talk all day long on call

2. My partner always makes me feel special

3. My partner and I support each other in every way

4. My partner and I heal together

5. My partner and I always makes the same core choice

6. My partner is always rooting for me

7. My partner just kissed me on my nose

8. My partner is so very adorable

9. My partner is kissing me at core. The core is the deepest root of our existence we can fathom .

10. My partner has confirmed within & out

Stage 44 : Writing my story

1. My partner loves me from the core of their being

2. My partner loves to surprise me every now and then

3. My partner and I share a very deep connection of oneness

4. My partner gets turned on by the very idea of my presence

5. We are daring to drop all the resistances to unify now

6. Our love is writing a historical tale

7. We are the miracle magnets

8. My partner and my heart are married to each other

9. My partner's heart is beating for me literally at the core

10. My partner and I daringly choose this union now at the core of our being

Stage 45 : Ten of cups

1. Harmoniously we are a happy family now

2. We went through a lot of hurdles but we finally unified now

3. I'm happy to see we have healthy children and a family

4. We are very content and satisfied

5. We are living the life of our dreams

6. Everything is perfectly founded forever

7. We are living the life we always wanted to live

8. All our dreams came true

9. We were the ones we were waiting for

10. Thank you God for such a miracle

Stage 46 : We got this

1. It all along was about reaching to this state of consciousness

2. It feels so good to be able to feel this love

3. I am glad you finally chose me

4. The reconciliation was a choice

5. I love how everything worked out for the highest good

6. Finally I feel complete peace, harmony and love within

7. Suddenly my life just transmuted

8. I feel ecstatic, free and relaxed

9. I am permanently out of the anxious restlessness

10. I am completely in a state of harmonious alignment

Stage 47 : Changing the momentum

1. Love has created a new history today

2. In love we are moving ahead

3. Everything heavy is falling apart from the core of our being as we now rise as one

4. I have always loved you and only you

5. We were always waiting for this union

6. We have come a really long way

7. We deserve this harmonious union

8. We are the love of each other's life

9. We will always choose each other beyond every temptation

10. We have been designed to be in this relationship and have received this reunion at this particular point in time. This is the divine timing we were waiting for

Stage 48 : We are all in this together

1. This story was meant to finish in this way

2. What God starts in us, he does finish it in His time

3. It's time for an overnight miracle

4. Magic is a part and parcel of life

5. My partner is now in the same room as mine

6. It's not exciting but very natural a feeling to be with my partner now

7. It's only with my partner that I truly fit in with

8. My partner and I are exploring the world together, inside & out.

9. My partner and I are in love creating history now

10. My partner often has realisations and epiphany that makes them feel extremely proud to have chosen to be with me once again

Stage 49 : The Miracle Happened

1. The miracle did happen

2. I am with my partner now

3. I am the one who is in a relationship with my partner

4. I am the one with whom it worked out with my partner

5. I am the one my partner has chosen to be with

6. I am the one who is now once again in a committed relationship with my partner

7. I am in a relationship at this very moment

8. I feel absolutely secure in this relationship

9. This relationship is the exact kind of relationship that I was always looking for

10. My partner has miraculously showed up for me

Stage 50 : We're back

1. I feel so good to post on social media with #weareback #reconcilliation #missedyou #loveofmylie #thankyouforcomingback #iloveyou #youremine #onlyloveisreal #lovewins #thankyougod #thankyouangels #thankyoutomyself

   #thankyoutoyou #thankyoutothislove

2. We just went to a trip together to recollect old memories and talked our heart out and it has lasted forever, we are still in this trip

3. We are creating magic together

4. Our love heals every fear

5. We are always in oneness

6. Love has chosen us at the very core

7. We are in union now

8. Our union was a matter of choice

9. Beyond all that's we chose each other

10. It's the most practical and logical step for us to be together because we're extremely compatible, can be ourselves with each other, so going out of our comfort zone to choose this kind of deep commitment at the core wasn't easy but we did it anyway – so we can truly grow freely in this authenticity, rawness and vulnerability. How we are in love, it reflects in every other sphere of life too

We are perfect for one another and so is every other aspect of our life. Thank you God

Conclusion

A self help book it is that challenge you to and overcome self limiting beliefs through the positive statements that have just penetrated through the core of your being

If you believe in the phrase "you are what we think", then life truly stems from your thoughts. But we cannot rely purely on thoughts; we must translate thoughts into words and eventually into actions in order to manifest our intentions

Affirmations are proven methods of self-improvement because of their ability to rewire our brains. Much like exercise, they raise the level of feel-good hormones and push our brains to form new clusters of "positive thought" neurons

In the sequence of thought-speech-action, affirmations play an integral role by breaking patterns of negative thoughts, negative speech, and, in turn, negative actions.

"You must assume the feeling of the wish fulfilled until your assumption has all the sensory vividness of reality. You must imagine that you are already experiencing what you desire. That is, you must assume the feeling of the fulfilment of your desire until you are possessed by it and this feeling crowds all other ideas out of your consciousness." -The Power of Awareness

"Dropping off to sleep feeling satisfied and happy compels conditions and events to appear in your world which confirm these attitudes of mind. "-Feeling Is The Secret Neville Lancelot Goddard generally known simply as Neville, was an American author who wrote on the Bible, mysticism, and self-help. Neville came to the United States to study drama at the age of seventeen. During his entertaining tour in England as a vaudeville dancer and stage actor, he developed a great interest in metaphysics. Hence, he gave up his entertainment job and devote fully to the study of metaphysics and spiritual matters. Neville gives the readers the necessary tools to understand and manifest what they desire in their lives. According to Goddard, the stories of Esau and Jacob, sons of Issac, are a metaphor of the method by which men manifest their desires.

Here are some of his quotes and book recommendations before I conclude

Mastery of self-control of your thoughts and feelings is your highest achievement. -Feeling Is The Secret All of us can realize our objectives by the wise use of mind and speech. -Seedtime and Harvest

You, by your conscious assumptions, determine the nature of the world in which you live. Ignore the present state and assume the wish fulfilled. Claim it; it will respond. -The Power of Awareness

There is nothing more fundamental to the secret of imagining than the distinction between imagining and the state imagined. -The Law and The Promise

Whatever the mind of man can imagine, man can realize. All objective (visible) states were first subjective (invisible) states, and you called them into visible by assuming the feeling of their reality

Once man accepts thinking from the end as a creative principle in which he can cooperate, then he is redeemed from the absurdity of ever attempting to achieve his objective by merely thinking of it. – Awakened Imagination

It might take a moment or a year – it is entirely dependent upon the degree of conviction. As doubts vanish and you can feel "I AM this", you begin to develop the fruit or the nature of the thing you are feeling yourself to be. -Your Faith Is Your Fortune

Truth depends upon the intensity of the imagination not upon external facts. Facts are the fruit bearing witness of the use or misuse of the imagination. -Awakened Imagination

The acceptance of the end automatically wills the means of realization. – Feeling Is The Secret

Change your conception of yourself and you will automatically change the world in which you live. Do not try to change people; they are only messengers telling you who you are.

Revalue yourself and they will confirm the change. -Your Faith Is Your Fortune

The world is yourself pushed out. Ask yourself what you want and then give it to yourself! Do not question how it will come about; just go your way, knowing that the evidence of what you have done must appear and it will. -Imagining Creates (Lecture)

To attempt to change the world before we change our concept of ourselves is to struggle against the nature of things. -Out of this World

Your world is your consciousness objectified. Waste no time trying to change the outside; change the within or the impression; and the without or expression will take care of itself. -Your Faith Is Your Fortune

In the beginning was the word. We create our own reality. It's all a matter of choice.

Make this your daily mantra to attract the relationship to your life

"I deserve to be loved unconditionally. I am honest, trustworthy and truthful in my relationship. I let go all the grudges and resentment.All my relationships are healthy, wealthy and divine. All my family members, neighbours, friends, relatives and even every living being love and support me very much! I accept myself as I am! I cherish amazing connection with optimistic, confident and uplifting people! I pay attention closely with my open heart when interacting with others! I have an amazing power to forgive myself and others fully! I am ready to receive love. I deserve love! I love and cherish the relationship with my friends and family members!All my activities lead me to a positive outcome! I open my self for the help from the universe and universe is sending it to me! I easily pay attention and trust my intuitions! I choose to live an enjoyable and happy life! I am blissfully and thankfully enjoying the wonders in my life right now!

I believe that my higher-self is sending me the best solution to the concern in my life! Thank You Archangel Michael for cutting every cord from the past, Thank You Archangel Raphael for healing my heart. Thank You Archangel Uriel for always giving me new and fresh ideas. Thank you Archangel Ariel for all the abundance. Thank you Archangel Metatron for cleansing every chakra. Thank you to the land of fairies and herbs of witches and shaman for healing every disease. Thank you Archangel Chamuel for such long term stability in every sphere of my life. Thank you God for the infinite possibilities and realms. Thank you Jesus. I love you"

The outer world is a reflection of the inner world. We are always attracting a physical reality that's is in absolute coherence to our current reality. What you truly realise within is what you manifest every moment. Every moment is a realisation and you are capable of realising anything. Every time you are upset, ask yourself what upset it's, what limiting belief do I have surrounding to this aspect that's not letting me see how it can transform to transmute to a state where it's in a state of coherence to create the vibration at the core which ultimately leads to get me what I want? The limiting belief is the resistance when you observe to realise that it doesn't exist, you transmute it at the core to make it what you realise it to be. Don't be hard on yourself for problem of concern .Accept and understand there are limiting beliefs surrounding it which is why it's a problem. For example if you find out your partner is in another relationship. Then obviously that is hurting you. Focus on understanding why you feel hurt.. In this case it'll be because you probably think deep down you have lost them forever. Well you are thinking like that because it's a limiting belief, you think they cannot have a break up. Their new partner may soon just realise that they have nothing to do with them. They don't exist. They are realising that they had nothing to do with them in the first place, ultimately this is leading to everything working out and you are in a relationship with the person of your desire. This how you change the story by always keeping a check of how you are feeling from time to time when you are living in the state of wish fulfilled where you act as if it's already done. So let's dive deeper with another example, you may think that they won't call, that's why you are upset. You may feel this doesn't work and everything has come to an end, you were born to suffer at the core level. However you may feel instead that all the hurt, all the pain, they have fallen apart and they were but creating a momentum for you for preparing you for this magnificent moment where you already have received a call from your person. In fact now the two of you have reconciled. All barriers moved apart making a way for you two and through the lens of your heart you can see each other once again. This is a way how you can move these situations to manifest. For those of you who got back in contact but seek deeper commitment, here's another example, what's making you upset and you were realising it was more about the inner union than having the person, you seek emotional intimacy or alignment of perspective. So what you are focusing on here is the problem that you don't have the kind of commitment that you seek, it's making you sick instead in your heart. You feel sometimes it better to not have it at all than to have it manifested halfway through. Well at the core you realise that the problem is there because you think it exists but instead you can also feel that miraculously it got resolved overnight and you have reached a state of realisation in your heart where you understand and believe that you have the kind of commitment that you seek and in that belief you have geared the strength to see through the lens of heart to believe , feel, realise and understand that you are the person who has received the kind of commitment that you seek . No matter why you are upset, find reasons to shift to state to etch a story in your heart that makes you see the possibility that you prefer.Aligning to the possibility believe that you have received what you seek. When you absolutely believe with no doubt you reach that state where your desire push through your vessel to become caricatures of character to live the role you assigned them to play. You are always creating your reality. Everything outside of you is a reflection of what is within . At the core what you believe to be obviously normal that manifests. Therefore make this lifestyle your new normal, take the responsibility to unleash the power within. The potential was all along in you, choose to manifest the best version of who has the life that they desire and believe that it's absolutely normal for you to receive it, for unexpected transformations to happen, you are in allowance. Suddenly miracles can happen for you too. Miracles can just show up out of nowhere and it just happens. You can really get lucky, your dreams can really come true, you can be with the person of your desire in the exact way that you prefer. Exactly how you desire, in that way something amazing can show up in your reality. All your dreams can come true out of nowhere

I am. You are. We all are the Christ, Christ is the Christos, the crystalline body we embody which is connected to all that's . It's crystalline because it's capable of channelling,

healing, integrating information, knowledge, understanding from all parts of the cosmos, from all that's – we are start dusts, literally an extension of the source. It is at the very core, in the essence of your being YOU ARE CHRIST, I AM CHRIST, CHRIST IS THE WAY to the portal of the magical new beginning. The more we remember our nothingness in God, the more faster we can be all that's. The moment we catch the momentum of awareness that we are soul, we realise we can be anything, we are liquid molten delight of silver, golden, purple, turquoise, unicorn and but infinite hues of colour streams admired in one another held by our stories so vibrant. But beyond our stories, in the very core corner of our being we are always experiencing a breakthrough together synced to the collective harmonious synchronicity. Knowing it's in God and with the faith in God in your heart – in the core centre of your very being, everything is possible, your desires and wishes can come true in God & with God. Your promises are fulfilled by God. Thank you God. Amen .No matter what you have done or your person has done to you, if you want a union or not – regardless of that everyone deserves to be forgiven at the core. Choose to know that you are worthy of receiving the kind of forgiveness that lets you feel that you deserve this relationship now. If you have to forgive them, then do so. They too deserve to receive this forgiveness. Upon receiving the forgiveness , now choose to allow the core aspect of relationship and the idea of the two of you coming together, to receive the forgiveness to itself this very second , right now. Forgive the idea of second chance. Forgive the idea of receiving the second chance . Forgive the feeling of feeling deserving of this second chance, you'll naturally move into a state now where you feel that you have received this second chance now. It's now time now. You are the one who has successfully manifested this relationship once again and you are in this relationship now with the love of your life. You are committed now to the person of your dreams. You are in an absolutely aligned relationship with the love of your life and dreams. You dream has finally come true and now you are in the exact kind of relationship you always wanted with the person you wanted to be in a relationship with. It's done. So it's. Thus it shall be. Amen

The Escape Suffering Loop Exercise

Why am I suffering? I am suffering because I am choosing to suffer. Why am I choosing to suffer? I am choosing to suffer because I think there's no way out . Why do I think there is no way out ? I think there is no way out because I am stuck . Why am I stuck ?I am stuck because I am scared to break free? Why am I scared to break free ? I am scared to break free because I don't know how long term peace feels . Why don't I know how long term peace feels ? I don't know how long term peace feels because I am too used to suffering. Why am I too used to suffering? I am too used to suffering because I'm familiar to how it feels . Why am I feeling familiar to how it feels ? I feel familiar because I have always been in it . Why have I always been in it ? I have been in it because I feel comfortable being in it . Why do I feel comfortable being in it ? I feel comfortable because I love pain . Why do I love pain ? I love pain because pain has been consistently there in my life ? Why has pain been consistently there in my life? Pain has consistently been there in my life because I've have chosen pain to be there in my life . Why have I chosen pain? I have chosen pain because it's the end result of everything. Why is it the end result of everything? It is the end result of everything because I am conditioned to it . Why am I conditioned to it ? I am conditioned to it because I believe it has to be this way . Why do I believe it has to be this way ? I believe it has to be this way because I believe it cannot be the other way round? Why don't I believe it can? It cannot be the other way around because I am comfortable with what is.Why I'm comfortable with what is? I am comfortable with what is because I'm scared of the new. Why am I scared of the new? I am scared of the new because of the preconceived notion that ultimately everything hurts. Why do I feel ultimately everything hurts? I feel everything hurts because it has been that way so something new cannot happen. Why do I feel something new does not happen. Why do I feel new things don't happen? I feel new things don't happen because new things are good and good things don't happen. Why don't good thing happen? Good things don't happen because I am not good. Why am I not good? I am not good because I am not loved. Why am I not loved? I am not loved because I am choosing not to be loved. Why am I choosing not to be loved? I am choosing not to be loved because I think I am not good enough. Why do I think I'm not good enough? I think I am not good enough because I am in pain. Why am I in pain? I am in pain because I am choosing not to come out of this pain. Why am I choosing not to come out of this pain? I am not choosing not to come out of this pain because I think I deserve this pain. Why do I think I deserve the pain? I think I deserve the pain because I have it for far too long. Why did I have it for so long? I have it for so long because I am choosing not to let go of it. Why am I choosing not to let go of it? I am choosing not to let go of it because it will come back in double I presume. Why will it come back in double? It will come back in double because it always does and then triples. Why will it multiply? It will multiply because it always does. Why does it always multiply? It multiplies because I choose it to multiply. Why do I choose it to multiply? I choose it to multiply because I don't know how life would be without it. Why don't I know how life will be without it? I don't know how life will be without it because I have not chosen to experience it. Why have I not chosen to experience it? I have not chosen to experience it because I don't think it's possible to have a pain less life. Why don't I feel it's possible to have a painless life? I feel it's not possible to have a painless life because I don't know how to replace pain with happiness. Why don't I know how I can replace pain with happiness? I don't know how to replace pain with happiness because I am scared to feel good. Why am I scared to feel good? I am scared to feel good because I am scared to receive love. Why am I scared of receiving love? I am scared of receiving love because I have got hurt in the past. Why have I got hurt in the past? I have got hurt because I have chosen to feel and remain hurt. Why have I chosen to feel and remain hurt? I have chosen to feel and remain hurt because I don't think I'm good enough to feel good. Why don't I feel I'm good enough to feel good? I think I am not good enough to feel good because I am not loved. Why am I not loved? I am not loved because I'm choosing not to be loved. Why am I choosing not to be loved? I am choosing not to be loved because I don't think I deserve love. Why don't I think I deserve love? I think I don't deserve love because I don't have the right to expect love from someone. Why don't I have the right to expect love from someone? I don't have the right to expect love from someone because expectation is wrong. Why is expectation wrong? Expectation is wrong because I have been made to feel bad for expecting. Why was I made to feel bad for expecting? I was made to feel bad for expecting because my expectation was not fulfilled. Why was my expectation not fulfilled? My expectation was not fulfilled because I didn't choose to allow it to be fulfilled. Why didn't I choose to allow it to be fulfilled? I didn't choose to allow it to be fulfilled because I didn't feel deserving. Why didn't I feel deserving? I didn't feel deserving instead I felt that I had to endure the relentless suffering because I am a sinner. Why am I a sinner? I am a sinner because I have sinned. Why do I think I have sinned? I think I have sinned because I have made terrible mistakes . Why have I made terrible mistakes? I have made terrible mistakes because I was hurt and expecting. Why was I hurt and expecting? I was hurt and expecting because I deserve to expect. Why do I feel I deserve to expect? I feel I deserve to expect because everyone deserves to expect and I'm good enough. Why do I think I am good enough? I think I am good enough because I have a beautiful heart. Why is my heart beautiful? My heart is beautiful because I love with pure consciousness. Why do I love with a pure consciousness? I love with a pure consciousness because I maintain a pure conscience. Why am I in a pure conscience? I am in a pure conscience because I am truly repentant. Why am I truly repentant? I am truly repentant because I deserve to be forgiven. Why do I deserve to be forgiven? I deserve to be forgiven because my intension is pure. Why is my intension pure? My intension is pure because I am a pure hearted soul. Why am I a pure hearted soul? I am a pure hearted soul because I have chosen to be one. Why have I chosen to be one? I have chosen to be one because I really love and care from a pure heart and consciousness and I'm good enough. I don't deserve to suffer but to forgive, forget and be forgiven and forgotten for the past mistakes to now give my self in God a second chance for this new beginning to have my manifestation exactly how I desire. Why will I received it exactly how I desire? I will receive it exactly how I desire because God loves me. Why does God love me? God loves me because God loves everyone. Why does God love everyone? God loves everyone because we are children of God and are one. Why are we one? We are because we are one in God. Why are we one in God. We are one in God because we are God, God is all that's, we are one in God. We are the essence of being and that's God. It is the state of our ultimate beingness. We can be anything because God can be anything and the very state of our very being is God. In the state of this very being we can choose to be love, be free, have the love exactly how we desire and now nothing can come in our way. I consciously now choose to be love and allow the breakthrough to happen because I feel completely in the momentum to feel good and strong enough to deserve it now.

It's done. Amen

Ezikiel 36:26 " And I will give you a new heart, and a new spirit I will put within you. And I will remove the heart of stone from your flesh and give you a heart of flesh."

Promises of the Lord

God promises to hear our lamentations

1. Psalm 10:17 You, Lord, hear the desire of the afflicted; you encourage them, and you listen to their cry.

2. 1 John 5:14-15 This is the confidence we have in approaching God: that if we ask anything according to his will, he hears us. And if we know that he hears us—whatever we ask—we know that we have what we asked of him.

God promises compassion.

3. Psalm 116:5-6 The Lord is gracious and righteous; our God is full of compassion. The Lord protects the unwary; when I was brought low, he saved me.

4. Peter 5:7 Cast all your anxiety on him because he cares for you.

God promises comforts.

5. John 14:16 And I will pray the Father, and he shall give you another Comforter, that he may abide with you forever.

6. 2 Corinthians 1:3-4 Blessed be the God and Father of our Lord Jesus Christ, the Father of compassion and

the God of all comfort, for who comforts us in all our troubles, so that we can comfort those in any trouble with the comfort we ourselves have received from God.

God promises faithfulness.

7. Psalm 9:10 Those who know your name trust in you, for you, Lord, have never forsaken those who seek you.

8. Isaiah 25:1 Lord, you are my God; I will exalt you and praise your name, for in perfect faithfulness you have done wonderful things, things planned long ago.

9. 1 Thessalonians 5:24 The one who calls you is faithful, and he will do it.

God promises to bring good out of suffering.

10. 2 Corinthians 4:17 For this light momentary affliction is preparing for us an eternal weight of glory beyond all comparison.

11. James 1:2-3 Consider it pure joy, my brothers, when you encounter trials of many kinds, because you know that the testing of your faith develops perseverance.

12. Galatians 6:9 Let us not become weary in doing good, for at the proper time we will reap a harvest if we do not give up.

God promises goodness.

13. Psalm 27:13 I remain confident of this: I will see the goodness of the Lord in the land of the living.

14. Psalm 86:5 For You, O Lord, are kind and forgiving, rich in loving devotion to all who call on You.

15. Psalm 119:68 You are good and do good.

God promises to guide us.

16. Psalm 32:8 I will instruct you and teach you in the way you should go; I will counsel you with my loving eye on you.

17. Proverbs 3:5-6 Trust in the Lord with all your heart and lean not on your own understanding; in all your ways submit to him, and he will make your paths straight.

18. Isaiah 48:17 This is what the LORD says– your Redeemer, the Holy One of Israel: "I am the LORD your God, who teaches you what is best for you, who directs you in the way you should go."

God promises hope.

19. 1 Peter 1:3-4 Praise be to the God and Father of our Lord Jesus Christ! In his great mercy he has given us new birth into a living hope through the resurrection of Jesus Christ from the dead, and into an inheritance that can never perish, spoil or fade. This inheritance is kept in heaven for you.

20. Jeremiah 29:11 For I know the plans I have for you," declares the LORD, "plans to prosper you and not to harm you, plans to give you hope and a future.

God promises to always love us.

21. 1 Corinthians 13:8 Love never fails.

22. Psalm 103:17 But the loving-kindness of the LORD is from everlasting to everlasting on those who fear Him, And His righteousness to children's children.

God promises peace.

23. Isaiah 26:3 You will keep in perfect peace those whose minds are steadfast, because they trust in you.

24. Philippians 4:7 And the peace of God, which surpasses all understanding, will guard your hearts and your minds in Christ Jesus.

25. Psalm 4:8 In peace I will lie down and sleep, for you alone, Lord, make me dwell in safety.

God promises to provide for us.

26. Philippians 4:19 And my God will meet all your needs according to the riches of his glory in Christ Jesus.

27. 2 Corinthians 9:8 And God is able to make all grace abound to you, so that in all things, at all times, having all that you need, you will abound in every good work.

God promises to be our refuge.

28. Psalm 9:9 The Lord is a refuge for the oppressed, a stronghold in times of trouble.

29. Deuteronomy 33:27 The eternal God is a dwelling place, and underneath are the everlasting arms.

God promises to restore joy.

30. Psalm 30:5 For his anger lasts only a moment, but his favour lasts a lifetime; weeping may stay for the night, but rejoicing comes in the morning.

31. Psalm 126:5-6 Those who sow with tears will reap with songs of joy. Those who go out weeping, carrying seed to sow, will return with songs of joy, carrying sheaves with them.

32. Psalm 94:19 When anxiety was great within me, your consolation brought me joy.

God promises to be our shield.

33. Psalm 84:11 For the LORD God is a sun and shield; the LORD bestows favor and honor; no good thing does he withhold from those whose walk is blameless.

34. Genesis 15:1 Do not be afraid, Abram. I am your shield, your very great reward.

God promises to sustain us.

35. Psalm 94:18 When I said, "My foot is slipping," your unfailing love, Lord, supported me.

36. Psalm 27:5 For in the day of trouble he will keep me safe in his dwelling; he will hide me in the shelter of his sacred tent and set me high upon a rock.

37. Psalm 3:5 I lie down and sleep; I wake again, because the Lord sustains me.

38. Jeremiah 17:7-8 But blessed is the one who trusts in the Lord, whose confidence is in him. They will be like a tree planted by the water that sends out its roots

by the stream. It does not fear when heat comes; its leaves are always green. It has no worries in a year of drought and never fails to bear fruit.

God promises to be with us.

39. Psalm 34:18 The LORD is close to the brokenhearted and saves those who are crushed in spirit.

40. James 4:8 Come near to God and he will come near to you.

41. Hebrews 13:5 ... God has said, "Never will I leave you; never will I forsake you."

And these are but the outer fringe of God's works! When we see how many promises God has made and how often He repeats them through scripture, we can stop fretting and trust God for all of our needs.

We are energy beings. You are vibing at a particular frequency. Just by choosing to vibe or vibrate in the frequency where you have manifested the exact version of your ex that you desire you can now be with your ex by choosing to vibrate in the frequency where you have chosen that . Just affirm " I choose to vibrate in the frequency where I have manifested my ex exactly just how I want and I also choose to believe that my ex is vibing in the same vibe . Therefore in this congruency , I choose to believe I have manifested the frequency where I am in a relationship with my ex once again exactly how I want . I choose to believe it's possible. Since it's possible to believe that I have manifested my ex . The version in which I desire my ex that is also a frequency. Therefore I choose to believe I have hacked and cracked the code of frequency that lets me now align to the state of consciousness where I have the frequency where I'm vibing now in the knowing that I have manifested the version of my ex into my physical reality exactly how I

desire . It's done . In Jesus's name .Amen

To pull someone's energy or a group of people's energy towards you, just focus on why you want to pull that , be clear with you intent, feel the presence of this energy in your heart, drop the resistance caused by desire, allow and make space to let what you desire, dropping the frequency of what you don't want(the resistance) you move to the frequency of what you do want(allowance/flow state) , as you hold it, your physical reality becomes a reflection of it, breathe in or pull in with love as you drop the resistance & now breathe out or push the love out into existence. Everyone is you pushed out. Be absolutely sure about why you want it and the characteristics, core values, ensure you have worked on every fear to reach a state of unwavering faith within (in your chest/heart/emotion centre of core feelings). In other words you have complete harmony and alignment in your heart centre. The angle of vertical and horizontal alignment is what is determining the precision of your manifestation. If it's at Christos or Christ or at state of perfect cross forming a perfect 360 degree and four 90 degree , at centre you'll feel absolute certainty. I AM CHRIST is the code when humbly affirmed with true intent from conscience, it shifts you immediately to a state of that being-ness. It's is in this complete stillness you receive exact manifestation. The word Christ is pronounced even in such a way, that if affects the presence of the barricades in the vortex &

immediately accelerate the momentum. You can have exactly what you want by choosing to relax and be in God. With God anything is possible. Nothing is right or wrong. What makes us feel guilty is our idea conditioned to it which makes us feel like we must feel guilty about it. The moment you realize to be repentant has nothing to do with feeling guilty but the intent matters. You move into a state of an observer. But where there is great grief in you in the morning and lamentation over the death of the old reality, you feel terrible because you cannot go back. But it's the association to an idea that for something to end means it's over. That's not true because to end means it's time for a new beginning. May people reunite. Those who truly want to reunite, do reunite . They desire with their true heart and soul. The fear you have beyond that choose courage. Tony Robbins says Courage is you have fear but do it anyway. He also says Fear is nothing but false evidences appearing real . Plunge in the courage to know amidst all the through awareness gathered through your reasoning that now you are shifting to experience in love, the most phenomenal breakthrough, ever . Each resistance is from a fear of loss. Fear or loss is from not having it or to be left with nothing. Where you are feeling the sensation of being scared in your heart, in that place , choose to remember that manifestation is real and it's safe to take a leap of faith. Where you scared that something bad will happen, choose that something good has already happened. Choose to believe in the absolute relaxation and state of being that nothing can go wrong anymore. What had to go wrong has gone wrong, now everything will go right. In love embrace this reasoning. Wherever you feel it's impossible you'll get so lucky. Understand you have incorporated to understand so much as you read the book slowly, with full focus and line by line, having to understand and to have implemented the teachings, in this process you have gone through a lot of transformation. May be you have reached out to me too by now for one on one sessions or courses or both. You have gone all in. It's a process and path of understanding & realising. You are realising your manifestation into existence. So it's not about alignment but absolute realisation, clarity, accountability and purity in your conscience which makes you feel worthy in the I AM CHRIST state in GOD. You have gone past the fear of persecution associated to CHRIST consciousness by moving past all those places where you had inner subconscious repentance, it was all making you feel unworthy. Finally you are in joy, laughing after what you just read and also realised. You'll never again punish yourself, however you feel true repentance to choose absolute forgiveness for yourself to choose no form of compromise , adjustment or giving up on the journey. You forgive yourself for torturing yourself in the past for making it compromise or feel like it has to. You are realising you don't have to. You are free to just be who you truly are without trying to fit in. You are here to create a new reality, a new world, a new earth. Now you are choosing to embrace who you truly are. In enormous gratitude, forgiveness, love harmony and joy we birth peace and reach a state of harmonious enlightenment where we choose the best for all. Everything is possible. All realities can coexist, what is true for me, might not be true for you. Neither of us are right or wrong. It's the different perspectives, the outlook or way of seeing life.

The perspective sets the rhythm. Choose to vibe with the state of consciousness where your manifestation has come true exactly how you desire. You are loved at the core of your being.

Stop trying to get your manifestation. I know you feel bad because you don't have them already and you love them a lot. But stop trying to get it. Instead the energy inside of you which is constantly trying to get it, doing something or the other to just get it somehow. Start to train your emotions that are feeling hopeless,anxious ,sad and are constantly trying to get it. Train them by consciously focusing on them from time to time & by telling them that you already have your manifestation now. Always ensure you are checking in, in your heart space. This book can be a great tool for you for that purpose,to get past limitations and manifest your dream. When you stop trying and start to practice calmness and relaxation, you vibration raises and also the vibration of your desire. You receive that same that you desire in a frequency where it has higher amplitude and purpose of existence integrated with a sense of realisation therefore having a solid foundation to be the base of your support to let you just be. We try from a place of lack – we are conditioned to try and put all in to be successful. However here the effortless you are, the more natural, relaxed and soul aligned you are, the faster you manifest. Don't be hard on yourself, radically love yourself. What you desire , desires you . What you seek is seeking for you . Ensure you are comfortable with receiving the manifestation. When your ex shows up once and you are not happy with that version. You can let that version go. Each time when you have done the inner work to reach absolute certainty you'll manifest them back. Be comfortable to receive your manifestation. If your manifestation shows up today, are you comfortable to receive it today? Are you comfortable to feel worthy of it in every way? Do have more forgiveness and self love to incorporate? Consider going to the part of you that feels uncomfortable to receive your manifestation, in your chest space, on the inside you'll feel it. In that part keep chanting I'm sorry. Please forgive me. I love you. Thank you. You can do the ho'oponopono meditation techniques too. Just look up on the internet. Just everyday see how comfortable you are to receive your manifestation and love that aspect gearing the strength to receive the miracle. Keep loving yourself unconditionally in that aspect within. In just receiving that love you'll experience miracles that you never even imagined of before. Your ex will show up, your life will level up and you'll start to truly feel more joy to receive more and more love everyday.

You'll keep getting more blissful and your life will be full of happiness and miracles forever. It starts with you. When you feel worthy of receiving your love in core aspect within, everything on the outside which is simply a holographic representation of the same loves you. Everyone is you pushed out. Everyone is an aspect within. Just by loving every feeling that any person or experience generate inside of you, in your heart space in the chest area where you feel it, you can heal that in you as well as in them. The entire world is crystal ball of love put in the centre of our hearts. Let us just unconditionally love all that is to get nothing but for the sake of it. Then we shall create a world that takes nothing but gives just for giving unconditional love. May love be the new currency. In love you can just be anything. Just be who you are in the madness of this deep love engrossed in it's intoxicated affair, getting fully overpowered by love. Giving up on every fear but knowing you create your reality, love every part of you that is scared to receive the kiss from the portal of magic. Love yourself even after you have infused yourself with all the magic to become a living embodiment of it. Immerse yourself in the radiating bliss of this love. Let this love penetrate through all the obstructions in your being holding you back from receiving this love. All resistances in your heart is there because you believe that you cannot receive this exact kind of commitment . But that's going away as the light of God intervenes and God gives you the chance now to show you the sky of clarity but through the lens of your heart. It's in this calmness you have reached a state of absolute oneness where you are now in a relationship with your ex once again, exactly how you desire. It was out of nowhere made possible in God. Congratulations you've made it to live in the wish fulfilled. It's done. I know this is probably the best book you have read and it's giving you the greatest sense of strength ever. I'm sure this will forever remain one of your most suggested and most favourite book ever. You deserve it. This book is your gift to you from your parallel self.However it was all along inside of you. God loves you. Love loves you . God is love. Love is all that's .

No one has the power to decide what is right or wrong for you unless you give that power to them. We give away the power when we have lost the sense of identity of who we truly are or have lost the vision to life and dreams. We have forgotten who we truly are within. We are powerful co creators, children of God, made in the image of God. We have God like power, strength and resiliency and pure unconditional love is the secret fuel. You can hire a coach to keep you up with the momentum, get spells or reiki to accelerate the momentum. You may have read many books, watched self help courses or videos. You may have read all the articles. But still you don't see results. Well it's about implementing your awareness into being. Become what you know and keep learning. One day you'll become the knowing that you are your manifestation & that is here. You keep growing, learning and evolving every passing day. Simultaneously keep finding ways to make the relationship better and better, honouring it and cherishing it finally that you have it once again exactly how you wanted. Responsibly honour the relationship, feel it's importance , sing songs of gratitude, Thank God for it, everything,for nothing and just like that. After all the pain and hurdles, you finally received the healing that lead to make you feel worthy enough to receive healing now to the extent that you feel worthy of receiving your manifestation. Your inner blocks are breaking apart and all the clogs are moving away and you can absolutely relax. Each clog in your wounded heart space are loved by God , each clog is breaking itself in half to receive this love from God to break apart. You may see a golden space in your heart that you are moving through. However that's because you have a heart of gold literally as a soul. At the very being the truth of awareness is inculcated in you that your ex has shown up in your consciousness now. Your this reality has nothing to do with the past or the pain or suffering or illness or guilt or regret. You may feel completely detached from it now. As if you are an observer. In that observation understand that the aspect of you which is on fire and is suffering in a state of risk and fear because that's shaking literally. As you choose to splash water on that fire. You will observe just a tiny cell in a cross over of tissues trembling. That little cell trembling is the state of being in you, the little tiny dot you could call it in a vast universe. As we observe the part of you trembling, we understand it's trembling because it feels it will not get the love that it desires. Something terrible will happen instead and it'll lose it all. This is where the flight or fight syndrome, state of desperation, state of lack or you will not have your desire states of consciousness are active. The reason is of course you are scared something terrible will happen. The fear is there as already a lot of terrible things have happened which is why you are reading this book. Along with that too many more things have happened simultaneously much coincidentally or something terrible might have lead to the break up. Meanwhile nothing is a coincidence. Everything is happening in perfect order and timing. The part of learning manifestation and freeing yourself from tremendous suffering was destined for your soul's path of flow. So you are scared because in the past things went wrong. Now automatically you'll observe you are no longer shaking on the inside all that much. You are comparatively just being. Meanwhile you may still not completely be at ease and are anxious, well it's to revise and remember that you create your own reality and manifestation is real. Finally you can let go and something just freed itself from you. You had a breakthrough Some of you may still have a layer of fear still holding you back and in this state, at the core of your being, you are trembling, we remember once again that you are indeed a child of God. In God anything is possible , taking a leap of faith it's time to let go. You have taken the ultimate leap of faith now and have reached a state of peace. You are now in the world of imagination & creativity- in this reality where you live a reality where dreams have come true, it is a reflection of your true state of being where at the very core you are vibrating in true joy, epiphany and peace. You have received your exact manifestation. Suicide or death is a conclusion of your limiting beliefs. Why will you choose death when you are already dead? You are already dead in this dreadful pain. What if you could choose to be freed from this pain by choosing to create magic and imbibe in these information to now create the life of your dreams. Don't even think of quitting. The pain is seated in the essence of your being. Your being is the extension of your soul. You cannot escape the pain by taking your life away. The pain is the yearning in your essence of being at the very core. If this break up makes you have the thought of taking your life away, at the core keep loving yourself until you reach and even beyond the realised belief of it's possible to manifest your exact desire, choose to receive a breakthrough at the core. When you can believe, it can manifest because it'll be a natural reception to the rhythm of your life syncing to the course of your being something that your heart is relaxed to envision. This life is beautiful and full of possibilities you will readily exclaim! Magic is indeed very real, so is God! What you know to be true and possible with absolutely certainty creates a momentum which manifests.

When you are at ease, you feel safe. When you feel safe, you can relax. When you relax, you can relax every neurotransmitter causing a sense of clogness in fear to release itself and relax in absolute expansion at the very core. The more this relaxation grows, in every part of your being, you break free more & more. In the very core existence you find the serendipitous liberty. This is the true liberty, a higher sense of conscious freedom that gives you the true freedom or permission slip to be just anything that you prefer . In this liberty you are eligible to have literally everything. From the very core heavy burdens are now lifted. Each resistance is there as long you think they exist. Therefore extremely in the most logically equipped understanding of awareness now let go of them. Each time they come around, consider reminding yourself that they are but just are limiting beliefs beyond them you have it all that you desire. Therefore now you are where your exact manifestation is, don't forget to check in your inner feelings and remind every resistance every now and then that they are merely limiting beliefs, you have your manifestation exactly how you wanted and these resistances were merely glitches catalysing the alchemy of this euphonious harmony of love, light and truth of your being. You have all that you desire, what doesn't let you believe or resonate is a limiting way of looking for a reasoning how it'll happen and when. It will happen by knowing that the resistance is a limiting belief which when is convinced it's possible, it will dissolve to equalise with the flow. The equalisation of all the sensation of barrier in heart when liquefy, a momentum is created or rhythm is created which brings you to the frequency of ease. It'll happen when you have learnt to be still and at ease beyond the fear and have persisted through the storm. You have believed fully at the core it's possible and it has happened. In this rhythm when your inner desire and outer reality are in absolute harmony even when you don't see evidences, suddenly out of nowhere when you least expect it'll show up. It'll be obvious then, you'll feel it, shall be bombarded with signs, angel numbers, feathers or even their names. This is when you'll be moving into the vortex of this reality slowly and as you move in. Eventually your rhythm will align to that and as a stream of it's extension, the very centre act as a projector with mesh reflecting to your reality, what you are being in this current vibration. Just by raising the frequency of the core of your being you can manifest your desire. Literally imagine a regulator in the core more aspect and you are increasing the amplitude by moving it in clockwise direction. As you go on increasing against the pain, pleasure flows in as light from the core of your being reverberates - through the lens of the projector or the eye of your heart- light is now coming out forming a prismatic effect . It's the warriors of the rainbow tribe energy that rise in you and you are breaking free from the old norms of living and being – creating a standard of living for your being and existence on earth. It's time to give yourself the chance to settle for love and marry the person you want to truly love and be with , from the core of your heart. You are free. Everything is possible and fair in this world and of course needless to say it's so also in love of course.

I've been talking to a lot of clients who had their share of success after doing my self help courses or one on one sessions . Well the #1 key to get back their exes was to completely let go and move on with no hope. I felt immediately I should share this with more people, so more lovers can come together. #2 key is to love and focus on yourself for the sake of loving yourself and not to get anything from loving yourself from the outside

So just understand that it has been a lot of time and there is no more hope left. Just let go of the hope, desire and all the wishes to be with your ex. Allow yourself to fully be in a state where you know that there's no point trying to manifest your ex to come back to you- there's no more hope remaining . It would be best if you let yourself move on . Just let it go now. Continue to do this and let it all go till you reach a point where you are hopefully hopeless or it no longer matters to you if your ex is coming back or not, you have understood, it's just not happening anymore in this lifetime perhaps

As you continue to be in this state sooner or later you'll reach a state of consciousness where you have accepted that they are not coming back anymore and you are unaffected about that completely. You are still doing the inner work, meditations to get them back but you are doing them just for doing them, for the sake of self love and inner satisfaction to feel really good & relaxed within, you have nothing to get out of those. You do them when you feel like, it just simply feels good to do them. You imagine things with your partner in a new version in a new timeline sometimes in flashes but not to get anything out of that . You no longer have a heavy heart. You no longer are longing. You have accepted the ending and have accepted that there is nothing you can do about it. It's over and everyday you are accepting it more and finding happiness for coming out of the heartbreak. You are happy to just breathe and be alive. You are beginning to finally find reasons to be happy for just being. Meanwhile at the same time you are also letting go and relaxing with the acceptance that what's lost cannot come back In this state you finally start to become a new version of yourself and align more to your ideal state of authenticity. You become more of who you truly are, get pulled towards new hobbies, ideas and beginning. This is the time when you start to love yourself truly, go on dates with yourself, spend more quality me time than ever. This is the time the wound is gone and you begin to relax more to find joy in this new beginning.

You start to feel so much love for yourself that you no longer need or want your ex or any relationship just for the sake of having a companion. You reach a state of consciousness where you can just relax to just be. You love your life and nothing else matters.

This is when in complete relaxation just for fun you can imagine that how things would be between you two if after all these months or years if you two would suddenly meet, how would things be. Who are you after all these years or months? What's your new lifestyle like ? Who are your new friends? What's your life like now? What all do you do to feel happy? What new hobbies are there in your life? How do you feel about these new hobbies?

What do you for your living?

In the state of single hood, are you really called to start a new relationship? Do you really want a boyfriend or girlfriend? If so what kind of relationship do you share with them? What is this new person like? What kind of lifestyle do they have?

How many of you while reading it felt extremely lonely and realised that by now you have not had a life in a long time of your own and it's rather time to give life another second chance? It's time to give yourself a second chance to live truly for yourself.

There is a new version of your partner that exists. Whatever he's or she's like now, the very next second, the very idea in you that this new version of your partner exists will release you out of suffering as you see everything flip just in a fraction of second to surprise you out of nowhere with this new version of your partner now. Choose to believe in your heart that no matter what you have gone through, you have gone through it for a reason. Maybe you are very hurt at this point of time and that is the reason why you are frustrated and hopeless. You are looking for a quick fix or immediate solution. You somehow need some kind of solution out of this.

Well there's a solution out of this. The solution is to understand that everything is energy. We are all at a particular frequency currently. We have a dominant vibration in this very moment energetically. Your emotions, feelings, thought, behaviour, understanding, action, wisdom and state of being determine that vibration.

When that vibration changes or how you feel, think , act, respond, understand, determine, realise, behave, analyse, integrate shift changes, you start to feel, behave and act very differently. Similarly your partner is also an energetic being and a version of them that is capable of existing in every frequency out of the infinite frequencies that exists in this universe. Whatever frequencies you can access, anyone else on earth is also capable of accessing. We are all beings of light. Who you prefer to be is a frequency, your partner or anyone is capable of being that. It's not impossible. It's science. The conscience that's conscious that resonates & has to change the orientation of it's vibration to align, that's God. God is capable of being stuck in extreme limiting beliefs causing fear – and also is capable of choosing & being the breakthrough and also being all that's. It all happens in God's will of allowance – of free will. We are co-creating with God all the time and yet we are God. God is all that's.

However the unique congruency is carried out by your unique core frequency of inner choice of who you wish to be now and deep inside. Your partner also has this free will. However at that very core too , in the deep choice they make deep within – a frequency of your partner exists where they are choosing the reality that you are choosing

Law of attraction isn't what you think you attract but you attract what you are a vibrational match to. To attract the new version of your partner, you need to focus on believing that their frequency has raised to shift to that stare of consciousness where your partner is exactly choosing the kind of relationship that you desire. Remember only love is real.

The resistances are making you withhold yourself from receiving what you seek. Instead of withholding back then energy in fear, choose to believe it's safe to trust and let go. It's safe to trust in God and let God in. Just loosen the tight grip or give up on the resisting feeling, that's what is means to withdraw & just be. Relax and release, your manifestation is already yours.

You don't have to do a technique or read the book or follow a particular routine unless you can really feel it and believe it. Your version of what's absolutely true for you manifests

Keep rehearsing your new story that it's absolutely true for you that your ex has shown up the way you desire. Immerse in it. Become it. Know it to the extent that it pushes out itself to become your physical immediate reality.

Purge, complain, cry, release, let it come out from all the places where you are suffering in. Lament as long as you desire. Feel whatever you are feeling until you are ready. A point in time will arrive when you are absolutely ready and then start the process of starting to change your self concept

Once you start many times you'll get upset, feel the downward spiral. Keep calm and continue to love yourself and trust in the process.

Fearlessly release all the old baggage that you are carrying, it is that constantly fearful and triggered state in you which is trembling. Fearlessly let go of all the storms within and you are safe to do so

Nothing had happened in the past or that which is happening now will be carried to the future. You are free from the root and source cause of this suffering. You surely don't have to manifest anything dreadful you are scared of. You are scared of it now because you experienced it in the past. However you are now choosing not to carry forward it to the future timeline. With this assurance, you just experienced a natural leap of faith within.

If you are scared of black magic or curse, know that no weapon formed against you shall prosper, God is breaking the spells that were casted against you to stop your success or to stop you from receiving this love, all curses, spells and breath of jealousy breathed into your relationship is being breathed in by God and God is breathing it out to create a new reality where all yours dreams have come true exactly how you wanted.

You can also maintain a journal where you write letters to your ex everyday. You can literally pour your heart out and share all that you would want to share. You can also prepare a beautiful welcome gift for your ex in advance where you can put all the letters and everything that you would want to share with them.

You can simply observe the resistance that you feel now in your heart or chest centre and breathe in the anxiety attached from the still trembling point of it (resistance) in your being. Hold the breath till you feel calm in your being & free from the resistance. Repeat this process to allow yourself to finally reach a state free from every resistance. This is a powerful breathing tool. You can also incorporate the 7-7-7 breath work technique. Simply repeat the same , while you breathe in for 7 counts, hold for 7 counts and release for another 7 counts.

You can also imagine light from the source or the very essence of your being, is moving through you. This light from core of your being is radiating through your anxiety, now calming in down completely that you can relax. Each time your mind takes over and the inner chatter begins that's not in your favour. These exercises will immediately calm you down.. No desire is too big or extravagant or impractical or small to the universe. Everything is a possibility to the universe and is possible. You can have anything that you desire. No compromise or adjustment is required. What you seek is seeking for you. Everything else will be taken care of. Nothing or no one other than you has free will in your universe. Your universe is inside of you. What you think or feel is freely your choice. Always choose to create a reality of ease in your favour by speaking it into existence.

Let go of the pain and the story you are strongly holding onto of what is or what has happened. Keep loving yourself and be kind to yourself. Letting go the old timelines is not going to be an overnight work to success.

Accept your emotions, understand where they are coming from instead of bypassing it. Bypassing will store it as a subconscious thought which you may numb out to so much that you don't even feel anymore. Really be brutally honest to yourself throughout the process, it'll help you to keep going. Never suppress your desires and feelings, you can never be at ease in that state. Don't try to fit in. A lot of people suffer sometimes only because they are trying to fit in. You don't have to be certain way to be accepted.

Your partner in the new version wants exactly what you want. They love, accept and align with you where you are. Don't try to squeeze and fit in , in an infinite universe with infinite possibilities. Sky isn't the limit but the idea that sky is the limit in your self concept, makes it so. We've gone beyond to the moon and other planets, UFOs have been seen and we are in the end times when we are entering the golden age as humanity when in some years we shall remember who we are as gods and goddesses.

Don't limit yourself in this buffet of unlimited possibilities. You can be here, there, everywhere, do anything. Play in anyway that you desire. We are in a playground, we're all playmates and you decide who you are going to play with in your universe and what game you'd want to play. In your universe , only you exist. You can make believe anyone to be your playmate and what you are make believing for their role to behave like is up to you. Pretend to believe your ex is giving you the exact kind of commitment in the playground of life. This is a game. There is nothing right or wrong, dark or light in this game, the story line and plot can be anything. If you feel guilty, well you are role playing that you are guilty and you are being punished. This is a terrific fetish that seem to be turning on the vast majority of human population, which is often enacted as a role of people playing to suffer and feel destiny or luck is against them. If you feel guilty about the third party , (in case someone is there in between you two) well in this case you feel pleasure in seeing your man or woman with someone else because it turns your wounds on to feel the pleasure of sacrifice to feel good about giving this love unconditionally. Plato would call it the Ludus stage of love , this as the stage of " ludus." It's in Plato's theory the stage of "pragma" or the stage when after exploring we are ready to settle, finally the reconciliation happens. Freudian psychoanalysis technique can be a great way to check your guilty pleasures. Sometimes we choose suffering on this journey because it creates a sense of pleasure causing heart to have orgasmic revelation which leads to a state of absolute transformation & the shift which leads to a great epiphany. Great is the realisation that the deepest wound is a fetish of self torture coming from this deep heartbreak where for many of you, each layer of suffering is causing a strange form of pleasure to keep you in feeling of the pain and this happens to an extent where finally through this pain you feel that absolute point of alchemy at core of your heart, where all the pain changes to absolute pleasure at the core to the extent that in that alchemy a shift happens and this is the quantum leap that happens when at the core of your being, immediately the reality flips, there's a timeline jump and you metamorphose to a new way of living where you literally feel, like now you are, that your manifestation has already happened. It's a feeling that feels like the absolute truth of reality that it is done.

Eventually you'll reach a state where you can completely forgive yourself or your partner or the situation or anyone involved to the extent where you are ready to let go and completely believe in every aspect within that you are but ready for another chance, a new beginning.

The seven types of love in Plato's theory and it's correlation to the path of manifesting your ex back :

Eros Love of the body. This is where it started. The both of you felt a great sense of attraction towards one another. This is the eros stage, the journey where attraction brings you two together

Philia Affectionate love. This is when both of you began to feel affection towards each other and the friendship and strong bond is created

Storge: Love of the Child. This is when both of you start to get possessive about each other, get protective, vulnerable and the authenticity shows up. This may lead to disagreements – forming the layer to explore outside

Agape: Selfless Love. This is when unconditional love, space, need for personal space, need to explore more comes in because the inner child is still searching for the true authenticity

Ludus: Playful Love. This is the stage that often lead to taking breaks, losing interest, flirting, cheating jealousy, detachment. This is when love is being sought outside. We are healing. This is when healing journey or dark knight of the soul, soul searching , codependency, belief clearing, suffering reveal their existence of being within.

Pragma: Long-lasting Love. Finally the phase when after soul searching you realise the kind of commitment and settlement you seek. This is reached usually from a desire to settle from a sense of security and also companionship. This is also when you get very clear about exactly what kind of relationship you are seeking for. In this phase the characteristics matter more than the person of interest.

Philautia: Love for self. This is when you go within and finally give yourself all love beyond all that you have been through and focus on creating your reality into existence by choosing to receive the love you desire. This is when there is no settling for less but the go getter energy is fully activated and you absolutely choose to receive the love that you desire and are very specific about your desire with complete self love brimming out of your being as an extension of your very self

No matter how stubborn your ex is or if you feel they have moved on or if you feel that they are being manipulated or brainwashed or for their self respect or if for what they have been told- They can see through the many layers of manipulation now and in their heart they are choosing this relationship for love and beyond every barrier, people or what will society think, the truth that love has revealed to them at the core transformed everything and beyond all the question, answers and grievances they held, love is penetrating in & making them realise they've always wanted what you want. Their authenticity has unfolded from the core. At the very core space of fear coming from trying to fit in or to be a good person, they are choosing to be their real selves fearlessly and are relaxing to choose you and only you. All along you both were looking for that ideal best friend, partner in crime, one who you fight with like siblings, love each other like couples, gossip like sisters with and talk your heart out from the core and can be accepted as you are - your sense of right, wrong, good, bad are same- none of you judge each other but just love each other completely. – it's like they are your mirror looking back at you as your reflection. Bathing in this ocean of love - every barrier between the two of you fall apart and both of you unite in absolute oneness, harmony and love.

They are the love of your life, the gift from heaven and you are also the love of their life and gift from heaven. The two of are one and the same. All along it was about this deep love that you two share. You both love each other a lot and definitely do deserve this harmonious union.

Don't complain and whine about your current situation with your friends or family. Their reaction will make you feel more hopeless and confused. You may begin to wonder if even manifesting is even real or in that process because you'll take on many view points with their individual limiting beliefs, not yet programmed to the awareness of seeing through from the perspective of everyone is you pushed out.

Understand shifting to the new awareness is happening and can happen anytime. Faith it into existence. Keep believing it's already done. Don't continuously look for changes in your ex in the physical reality. The inner feeling , inner conversation, presence of being with your ex on the inside, reach you to a state where you so believe that it becomes your absolute awareness from within. You just know it's true for you inside and out . Trust and love the process. It's the knowing it into being that manifests. When you absolutely know it to the extent that you believe it to be absolutely true then it manifests as your absolute reality. As I write this, this particular realisation, I'm channelling from Lord Krishna now and I absolutely know , believe and feel it's true for me and so I am pushing it out as an information in my absolute reality. Like it's manifesting now. In same way when you know, feel, believe that you completely deserve your manifestation, it'll become your absolute reality that you push it into existence from within to without or in other words from inside to outside . Your inner reality pushes out when you feel deserving enough to receive it. In this state you relax to push out your inner understanding to an extent where after reaching a consciousness or state of being where you are so sure that the momentum is built up and an energy is created which creates a state of energetic consciousness within, which creates the momentum or force within which gets charged to an extent to have the absolute synchronization to gear in a state of consciousness where it's ready to push out. This is exactly how your manifestation shows up . You have complete control over your thoughts. Your thoughts manifest. Nothing outside of you can manipulate you to change your thoughts, unless you give power to it. You always have complete control over your manifestation. If you don't like something, change the feeling, story and thought associated to it, you'll immediately catch the rhythm of new thoughts immediately.

Now that you two are together, how are things between the two of you? What do you two talk about ? Where do you all go? What do you two do together? How's this new timeline like? How does it feel to be with your partner once again? How does it feel in the rhythm of your being to feel this feeling literally?

Remember always that God is guiding you and step by step & you are flowing and manifesting things into being.

You are the desire your desire is manifesting and all along you were doing everything in coherence to the movements of your desire. Your desire all along has been preparing you to receive your desire completely. Your desire is manifesting you and it's your desire's desire to unify the two of you, in peace, harmony, oneness, joy, epiphany, bliss and subliminal radiance of this enlightening unconditional love that unifies the two of you truly where you live in absolute authenticity. Breaking every barrier you two have now united completely within and so also on the outside. Only love is real.

Intentionally believe that you are worthy enough to receive your manifestation how you desire.

You have now received your manifestation. Your ex has finally shown up in your reality how you always wanted. It is safe to receive your manifestation how you desire, no one will humiliate you or try to take it away from you. No one will trigger you to take away what is yours. Those days are gone, you have worked on your self concept and you feel worthy enough to receive your manifestation now. You are the one who is breaking every barrier apart and are choosing this love at core of your being, to receive it now fully.

If you have a lot of resistances, read the core beliefs chapter of the book again. If needed read it a few times till you are ready to do the positive affirmations. It's safe to receive love. You are secured. You are protected. You are abundant. This love will not be taken away from you again. You can manifest it infinite number of times. You manifested it back, if you lose it again , you can again manifest it to your reality again & again – infinite number of times. There are infinite timelines ,lifelines & versions of you, everyone & of everything. No one can take away this power of manifestation from you. You can in fact let go of your desire again and again until your manifestation has shown up as exactly how you desire it be. Your manifestation all along has been yours. It was written in the stars even before you were born. You are meant to have this desire. You deserve this reconciliation with your ex. You have received what you seek. You finally have this relationship again & you are completely allowing yourself to receive this union in every core corner of your being. It's done. Be open to receiving more love and abundance.

Imagine opening in your heart space, as the blocks are falling away. The ray of sun is flowing through your being and you are allowing the light of sun in your heart. Feel the warmth melting every resistance, continue to breathe in through the nostrils of your heart, as this light percolates in. It infuses with all that's and in the very core part of your being, you are opening up more and more to receive this light from the sun. This solar energy healing will cause the inner solar flare in you leading to the event of your manifestation to be visible to the eyes in the physical reality.

This is possible. It's happening now . The sunlight in your heart is being breathed in by every wound in you and all parts of you that were hurting, continue to feel immersed in this light as those parts are breathing in the intense light of the sun. As more light is breathed in by you, you are becoming a beacon of light. Each shadow in the rusted darkness is allowing healing as sun rays wash over them. You are now literally naturalising with the magic of nature to become an expression of love and light. The truth is who you are being now, the one who has received all the warmth of the sun to believe that you absolutely have your manifestation now exactly how you desire. Choose to only resonate to information that makes you feel and believe that you have received your manifestation exactly how you desire. How glad you must be feeling to wake up everyday next to your partner? Where are you? How does the room look? What do you see around? What's the colour of the curtains? What's the colour of the wall? How do you feel to wake up next to your partner ? What is your partner doing? What are you two wearing? How does everything look around ? How happy you are with each other? What is a day in your new life like? What do you two do for living? What activities or work are the two of you choosing to do together? Where are you located? What's your locality like? How happy do you two feel to spend time together? What all do you all do to spend time with each other? How does your person make you feel special? What's your language of love?

You are the one who is in same wavelength with your partner. You feel chosen. You feel safe. You feel this is possible. You feel at the core of your being very relaxed to completely believe this is really happening . Everyone is you pushed out. In the very core of your being you feel this is real and your partner is conforming exactly how you desire. The instant gratification is first integrated within. When you completely can believe at the core of your being that it's possible, your person will push out to show up. I intend all of you who are reading this to have your desires manifested. Your partner's new version has confirmed. You feel so filled with delight. You feel light and all the barriers are gone. What remains is you and the version of your manifestation pushed out(that you are being). Remember the past or present doesn't matter. Manifestation is a path of inner vibrational shifting that push out to become your external reality. What might hold you back is trying too hard to change things on the outside. You can't change what is on the outside. You can choose to observe in inside of you how you feel about it, understand the root core cause of it which usually goes back to your childhood. You can read my book Chronological Remembrance - A Guide To Inner Child Healing & Integration for more support in this matter. However beneath every core wound that leaves you forlorn, is ultimately a desire to be seen, heard, chosen, loved, understood and accepted. As you understand what that aspect of you on the inside is seeking, love that part of you. If a part of you for example is quivering in anguish to be accepted. Accept that part of you, give yourself the kind of love you seek from someone else. If you that part wants to be seen, acknowledge to see it, it may show you deeper fears of say – fear of loss. Understand there is a part of you in a fear of loss, acknowledge and reassure that part that you shall not lose anymore but shall just receive, win and will be loved now. Acknowledging that, love yourself in every core aspect of your being. If your partner is not exactly in the desired version, acknowledge the hurt it is causing. It may stream from the consciousness that things cannot be exactly the way you desire. Understand it's coming from a place of never experiencing something so out of the world prior to this. Acknowledge that state of being, reassure and make yourself understand that it's possible. Love yourself and acknowledge each wound, reassure and make that aspect understand as you'd explain to a child. Once this aspect of you can completely believe and relax at the core, the series of events will be arranged out of nowhere. Everything all along has been, will and continue to lead you towards your heart's desire. Your desire is from where your life flows. You have your desires for them to be fulfilled. Don't be scared something might show up that you may not like. Instead love yourself where the fear is generated, may be you feel you'll lose it all. Maybe you have lost it all. Now you have nothing more to lose. Things have gone worse than you ever thought and you feel a terrible wound. However the real game changer is in this moment. In that awful wound choose to receive love. Reassure that part with a spark of remembrance that we create our reality and that manifestation is real. You are not the victim of the situations. The situations can change any time. The outside circumstances don't matter. Everything exists in infinite frequencies, so you can choose to vibrate at a frequency where your manifestation has confirmed. Whenever you feel a conflicting pattern of thoughts, understand that the conflict comes from the forgetfulness in the knowing that you already have manifested your reality. Just know that you have already manifested your ex and work on strengthening the belief that you have manifested your ex already.

Imagine and anticipate that in next 48 hours your manifestation will confirm. You are ready to receive it exactly how you desire and in next 2 days you are the one who will experience a magnificent breakthrough. In next two days your life is about to change and transmute completely for good, how you wanted it to be, all along , in your favour because you choosing it now. Nothing has to ever go wrong again, nothing has to be against your desire. Everything that you desire, you can have that, without having to give anything for receiving that love. You are the one who is receiving this love now, at the core of your being. You are activated in love vibrational frequency and in unconditional love, beyond all your fear, the trembled part of your being is receiving more of this love that locking it in .In complete relaxation you are now infusing in this love. This love is streaming through your being and touching each part of you – as you receive this love now at the very core of you existence. It's this love that washes away every fear at the core your being and you are now receiving this love in an infinity loop. The love from the core is going in to create a crossover to move out to receive this stream of love imbibed in this rhythm to create the infinity loop of love in your heart. As this activates completely , in this activation , the core aspect of being is experiencing an energetic breakthrough or energetically your manifestation has already pushed out to confirm. You felt that sense of assurance now, to an extent that at the core – you have now taken this leap of faith. You don't have to feel bad. The reason you feel bad is because you resonate to what you desire cannot come true, deep down. Don't feel bad but understand you can feel good, knowing and relaxing to be aware of the fact that you can manifest anything. So you don't need to feel bad, where you feel bad, choose to feel good there, knowing all your wishes have come true.

Know that you are seriously freed from the loop of suffering forever. At the very core of your being you are perfect. You are now choosing your partner to see you as perfect. You deserve your partner to give you the kind of chance in love that you seek. You deserve your partner to be absolutely in your team. You deserve your partner to harmonise with you completely. You deserve all the assurance at the core of your being where God has already assured you this new beginning because your desire was placed in you by God. It's God's desire that the desire fulfils in you and therefore in God, every barrier is lifted and all that's in between is being shattered into pieces and are infusing to the stream and rhythm of life where only good things are now happening for you. This shall now be your new normal.

If you find yourself getting back into to triggers and pain. Understand what you feel is creating a reality which makes you feel an amplification of your feelings projected outward. Hold the point within where it hurts in your imagination and remind yourself you are creating your reality and choose to take back the power and control in your hand now. Clenching the tiny little spot in your chest reverberating in pain, in your fist energetically , makes that aspect often feel safe. In you presence of literally holding that point, try to understand the texture of that spot, how does it feel? What is the shape? What is the colour. At the same time remember that you create your reality. If you were scared of something and that has happened many times that means you have manifested it.

So remembering these, continue to feel that aspect in your hands, folded in your palm. Now slowly start rubbing it in between your left and light palm remembering you are a powerful co creator and you are rubbing the wish lamp now with ease and realising everything you are holding onto insistently. You are rubbing off the insistency. Whatever you are holding onto tightly you are periodically creating. Understand this you now loosen the grip. When you feel completely light in that spot, imagine breathing in all the anxiousness from that molecule and breathing it out as a wishful thinking of excitement where all your dreams have come true through that tiny molecule of magic. Now you know you are magic, only magic happens to you and for you in your reality and every multiverse in your favour. You are loved. The entire universe is now telling you that we love you, welcome home love. You are here. You are most welcome. This is your kingdom, it all along has been. The kingdom of love , light and truth. The truth is that you are a magical being with a superpower called love.

The season of harvest and season of planting seed are different. Your desire is the seed planted in you already and your life is unfolding everyday to be an absolutely authentic vibrational match to your desire. The moment you have absolute unwavering faith and can know completely more in the very aspect - in the core of your being – your manifestation shows up. The convinced conviction will catch the momentum to create vibration to break free leading you to your ultimate breakthrough where finally your partner's exact vibration confirms. Since the time you two separated, love has all along remained unified and is reminding you two that you both are already one and together. There's no separation.

It's merely an illusion, all along the two of you have been one. As you believe it more and are convinced at the core that you seriously cannot lose this love, this love has all along been yours, you gear up in the momentum to now claim this love and choose this love to be yours. Transcending all the hurdles you have manifested your person exactly how you desire. No matter what it looks like on the outside, everything is already happening in your favour to unite the two of you exactly how you desire. Your person has confirmed exactly as how you forever wanted. It's done. You are loved. You are receiving love and you are chosen, at the core of your being. You are love. Love is all that's. God is love. Love is the magic. Only love is real. What you feel about your manifestation has to be your focus. When you change your focus to believing that you have received your manifestation and feel that way, your assumption will create synchronicity and lead to bridge of incidents that ultimately lead to the grand event of your main manifestation showing up. It doesn't matter what your ex is doing, what decision they are making in the immediate physical reality. It does matter how you feel about it. When you can change your feeling and shift it to believing you are with the version of your ex that you desire, despite what evidences are available, when you continue to hold on to that belief and work on making these beliefs stronger, the bridge of events will lead to formulation of the very moment where you have received your manifestation exactly how you desire in the physical reality. Your only work is to strengthen the faith that you have already received your manifestation.

How will my thoughts travel to my ex and manifest them?

Your essence of being is a tiny dot ,a molecule. That molecular essence of your being is where the life force energy is flowing through you. It's the connection. That connection is what connects you to the source of all that's , GOD . Through God we are all connected . It's by the virtue of quantum teleportation, the quanta or amount of information you are sending to the molecular aspect of anyone, they are receiving that quanta of energy & that frequency is providing all the information . So send thoughts like your ex has already committed to you instead of you don't deserve to be chosen.

Quantum teleportation is a technique for transferring quantum information from a sender at one location to a receiver some distance away. While teleportation is commonly portrayed in science fiction as a means to transfer physical objects from one location to the next, quantum teleportation only transfers quantum information. The sender does not have to know the particular quantum state being transferred. Moreover, the location of the recipient can be unknown, but classical information needs to be sent from sender to receiver to complete the teleportation. Because classical information needs to be sent, teleportation can not occur faster than the speed of light.

Faith moves mountains.

Thank you for picking up a copy of my book and investing your precious time to read it. I really appreciate your effort. I will be extremely thankful to you if you could share your review and rating for this book on the platform from where you purchased this book . Other readers will always be interested in your opinion of the books you've read. Whether you've loved the book or not, if you give your honest and detailed thoughts then people will find a new book that maybe is also a right fit for them.

Exactly the way you desire – in that exact way your manifestation has confirmed. Manifestation is a muscle building exercise. This content created the momentum in you to catch the rhythm to create your reality into existence. The manifestation first shows up on the inside and then is pushed out to be visible. The unseen is manifesting itself into being seen. Adhere to persistency , resiliency and determination – you shall co create your exactly desired reality into existence. The exact kind of miracle and blessing you were looking for, that has shown up in your life now. You are the chosen one. You attract your desires into being. You are a magnet for miracles. You are loved beyond measure. You are blessed. Thank you God. I love you God. In Jesus's Name. Amen.

> ***Connect to me on Instagram:***
> ***@vibrations_and_alignment***
> ***Find out more about me:***
> ***https://www.quantumdynamic8.com***

www.ingramcontent.com/pod-product-compliance
Lightning Source LLC
LaVergne TN
LVHW050605200726

843508LV00010B/1778